CLIP & TELL

Some More

Bible Stories

By Lois Keffer

Group

Loveland, Colorado

Dedication

To the memory of my brother, Lowell Mack, who with incredible grace and courage
"slipped the surly bonds of earth and touched the face of God."

Clip & Tell Some More Bible Stories
Copyright © 1998 Lois Keffer

Credits
Book Acquisitions Editor: Jan Kershner
Editor: Jody Brolsma
Senior Editor: Paul Woods
Chief Creative Officer: Joani Schultz
Copy Editor: Julie Meiklejohn
Art Director: Ray Tollison
Cover Art Director: Jeff Storm
Computer Graphic Artist: Eris Klein
Cover Photographer: Jafe Parsons
Illustrators: Lois Keffer, Jan Knudson
Production Manager: Peggy Naylor

Library of Congress Cataloging-in-Publication Data
Keffer, Lois.
    Clip & tell some more Bible stories / by lois keffer
        p.   cm.
    ISBN 0-7644-2045-3 (alk. paper)
    1. Bible stories, English.   2. Bible--Study and teaching.
    3. Storytelling in Christian education.   4. Paper work.   I. Title
    BS546.K43   1998
    220.9'505--dc21

                                                                        97-43993
                                                                        CIP

10 9 8 7 6 5 4 3 2 1   07 06 05 04 03 02 01 00 99 98

Printed in the United States of America.

CONTENTS

NEW TESTAMENT

INTRODUCTION

Be a Great Storyteller!

Bible stories are a priceless treasure, relating the very foundation of our Christian faith. *Clip & Tell Some More Bible Stories* helps you combine storytelling with fascinating paper creations that unfold as you speak. As you lead children through the Bible, you'll have them on the edge of their seats!

But these stories from God's Word provide much more than entertainment. Old Testament stories tell about Bible characters whose faith and obedience to God molded history. The New Testament stories focus on Jesus' life and teaching. And each story emphasizes an important Bible truth that's reinforced though a memorable active-learning experience, an action rhyme, a song, or an opportunity for kids to make their own fold-and-cut Bible figures. Guided discussions help kids see how they can apply what they've learned to their own lives.

How Do I Start?

Clip & Tell Some More Bible Stories offers twenty-two stories from the Old and New Testaments presented in chronological order. You may want to teach these stories as a series or choose individual stories to use on special occasions.

Read each story in the Bible to familiarize yourself with its context and content. (You'll find Bible references in the Contents and at the beginning of each story.) A quick review of study-Bible notes or a Bible handbook or commentary will help you feel even more prepared and confident to answer any questions kids might ask.

What If I'm All Thumbs?

Not to worry. These simple fold-and-cut figures will have everyone thinking you're an artist! Use scratch paper to practice folding and cutting the figures until you're comfortable with them. When you present a story to a group, hold the paper with the blank side facing your listeners until the instructions direct you to display the figure.

Most of the stories have two or more figures. Make your storytelling as simple or elaborate as you like by using one or all of the figures.

Where Do *Clip & Tell Some More Bible Stories* Work Best?

Use these versatile stories in

- after-school programs
- banquets
- camp devotions
- children's church
- craft time
- midweek clubs
- Sunday school
- vacation Bible school

Or use them as the basis for meaningful, interactive family devotions.

Don't shortchange the adults in your congregation by assuming that these stories are only appropriate for kids. Try using them for intergenerational worship or even with an adult class. You'll find that kids of all ages are eager to see and hear familiar Bible stories presented in a new way!

Have You Thought of This?

You can use the figures in this book for much more than storytelling. You'll discover all kinds of creative ways to use them in your home or classroom. For instance, use them as clip art or to create stencils, puppets, or borders for bulletin boards.

If you're using the stories with preschool children, fold the paper you will use for the figures before class. You'll hold young children's attention better if you can start cutting the figures right away!

If you're using the stories with children in the elementary grades, you may want to photocopy enough patterns so that each child has a complete set. They'll love cutting and folding the figures themselves. While they work, you can review the story with them and ask how the things they learned in the story will help them live for God.

God bless you as you use this book. May these ideas bring your children hours of creative Bible learning!

Lois Keffer

OLD TESTAMENT

GOD CREATES THE WORLD

PREPARATION

Photocopy the crown pattern onto gold paper. The pattern for this story is on page 12.

THE STORY

✂ *Cut on the heavy lines around the entire pattern, and discard the edges.*

In the very beginning of everything, even before time had begun, the universe was dark and silent.

✂ *Cut from A to B. Lay the smaller section aside.*

God's Spirit moved over the misty water.

✂ *Cut from C to D. Set aside Section 4-5-6.*

Then God said, "Let there be light."

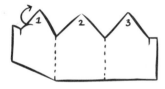

◺ *Fold back Section 1 so children can see the number 1, representing the first day of Creation.*

Suddenly a brilliant light flashed from heaven, and God divided the light from the darkness. God called the light "day" and the darkness "night," and that was the first day of Creation.

Then God said, "Let there be something to divide the water in two."

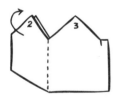

◺ *Fold back and display Section 2.*

So God separated the sea from the sky, and that was the second day of Creation.

Then God said, "Let the water under the sky be gathered together so the dry land will appear."

☞ *Display Section 3.*

And that's just what happened. God called the dry land "earth" and the water "seas." And God saw that it was good! Then God said, "Let the earth produce plants." And plants of every kind sprang up! Grasses, bushes, trees, and flowers of every color sprang up all over the earth. And God saw that all of them were good. That was the third day of Creation.

✂ *Open the figure and cut Slits 1 and 2. Lay Section 1-2-3 aside.*

Then God said, "Let there be lights in the sky to separate day from night."

◺ *Fold back and display Section 4.*

God made the sun to rule the day and the moon to rule the night. And God scattered billions of twinkling stars across the night sky. God saw that they were good. And that was the fourth day of Creation.

Then God said, "Let the water be filled with living things, and let birds fly in the air above the earth."

△ *Fold back and display Section 5.*

So God made whales and snails and fish in the sea and birds that fly through the air, wild and free.

God saw that all of them were good. And that was the fifth day of Creation.

Then God said, "Let the earth be filled with animals."

So God made bears and dogs and cats and cattle,

Horses and bugs and snakes that rattle.

God saw that all of them were good.

Then God said, "Let us make human beings in our image and likeness. And let them rule over the fish in the sea, the birds in the sky, the animals that live on the ground, and everything on the earth."

☜ *Display Section 6.*

So God made Adam and Eve. God saw all that he had made, and it was very good! And that was the sixth day of Creation.

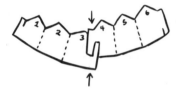

✂ *Open the figure and cut Slits 3 and 4. Slide Slits 2 and 3 together.*

Then God gave Adam and Eve a very special job. God blessed them and said, "Have many children and grow in number. Fill the earth and be its masters. Rule over the fish in the sea and over the birds in the sky and over every living thing that moves on the earth." God wanted Adam and Eve to care for the beautiful new world.

Now taking care of the world is our job, because we're sons and daughters of Adam and Eve.

△ *Fold back and display the "Creation Keeper" Section.*

I'm a Creation Keeper, and so are you! What are some things we can do to take care of God's creation?

☜ *Display Section 7.*

On the seventh day of Creation, God rested. God rested to set an example for us. If we're going to be good Creation Keepers, we need to rest and worship God one day out of each week.

✂ *Cut Slits 5 and 6. Slide Slits 4 and 5 together and then slide Slits 6 and 1 together. Place the completed crown on your head.*

People are the very best part of God's creation, because we can think and create things and love others. Because God made us so special, God trusts us to take care of the wonderful world he created. I hope you'll all be good Creation Keepers this week!

You may want to have kids cut, fold, and assemble their own crowns.

Then teach kids this lively rhyme.

Creation Rhyme

Daaaaaaa-y one!

God spoke in the darkness; he said, "Let there be light!"

(Cup your hands around your mouth.)

And just like that, there was day and night.

(Stretch your arms overhead with "twinkling" fingers.)

Daaaaaaa-y two!

There was water down below and water up high.

(Bend and push your hands low; straighten and stretch your hands high.)

Then God made the air, and he called it "sky."

(Wave your arms back and forth overhead.)

Daaaaaaa-y three!

Then up went the mountains, and down went the seas

(point up with your left hand; point down with your right hand);

And God made plants and flowers and trees.

Daaaaaaa-y four!

Then God created the sun so bright

(make a circle with your arms overhead)

And the moon and stars to shine at night.

(Make a smaller circle with your arms; flick your fingers so they "twinkle.")

Daaaaaaa-y five!

God made the creatures that swim in the seas

(put your hands together, and pretend to "zoom" through water)

And the birds that fly through the sky on a breeze.

(Tuck your thumbs under your arms, and flap your "wings.")

Daaaaaaa-y six!

God made the animals that walk, hop, and crawl

(crouch down on all fours);

Then Adam and Eve he made last of all.

(Have the boys bow and then have the girls bow.)

Daaaaaaa-y seven!

"Very good!" God said as he looked down from heaven.

(Give two "thumbs up.")

And then God rested on day number seven.

(Rest your cheek on your folded hands.)

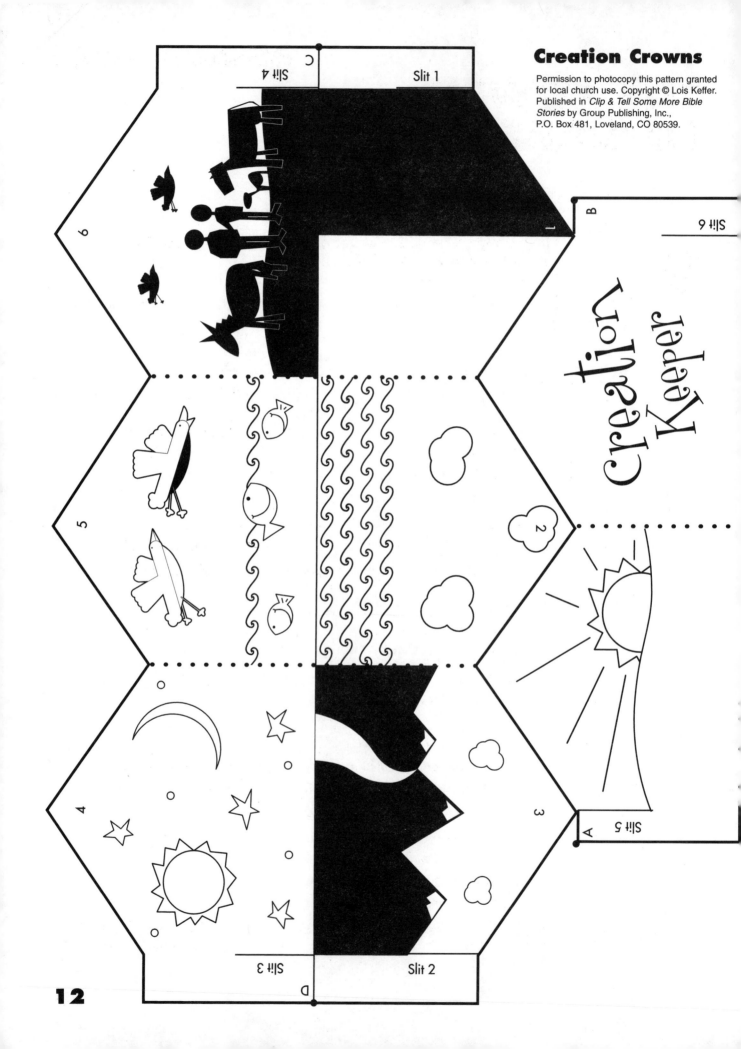

Creation Crowns

Slit 1

Slit 4

Slit 6

Slit 5

Slit 3

Slit 2

Creation Keeper

THE TOWER OF BABEL

PREPARATION

Copy Figures 1, 2, and 3 (the tower) onto gray paper. The patterns for this story are on pages 15, 16, and 17.

THE STORY

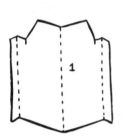

Fold Figure 1 in half on Line 1.

Long ago, while the world was still quite new, everyone spoke the same language.

Cut from A to B. Cut Slit 1.

One day, someone had a great idea.

Fold forward (mountain fold) on Line 2.

He said, "Let's make bricks and bake them so they're hard."

Open the figure, and fold the left edge forward to match the right edge. Set Figure 1 up beside you.

"Then we can build a city for ourselves."

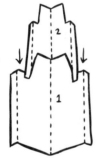

Fold Figure 2 in half on Line 1. Cut from A to B.

"Our city will be fine and big."

Cut Slits 2 and 3. Fold forward on Line 2. Open the figure, and fold the left edge forward.

"And we'll build a huge tower in our city."

Attach Figures 1 and 2 by sliding Slits 1 and 2 together, as well as the two "unmarked" slits on the left side. Set the tower up beside you.

"Our tower will reach all the way up to heaven!"

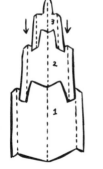

Fold Figure 3 in half on Line 1. Cut from A to B.

"Our tower will make us famous."

Cut Slit 4, and fold forward on Line 2. Open the figure, and fold the left edge forward.

God saw what the people were doing.

Attach Figures 2 and 3 by sliding Slits 3 and 4 together, as well as the "unmarked" slits on the left side. Stand up the completed tower.

God knew that these people were proud and stuck-up. They didn't love and obey God. They wanted to show everyone how smart they were. But God knew what to do to stop them from building the tower. God made the people start speaking different languages. Suddenly, they couldn't understand each other. Listen to this little poem, and repeat each line after me.

Babble, babble! What did you say?

Why in the world are you talking that way?

Your words don't make any sense at all!

Now how will we build this tower so tall?

So everyone stopped working on the tower because they all spoke different languages.

Let's try saying "hello" in different languages.

In French, people say "bonjour." Can you say "bonjour"?

In Spanish, people say "hola." Can you say "hola"?

German people say "guten Tag." Can you say that?

Japanese people say "konichi wa." Say that with me.

You just spoke five different languages, including English.

God created languages to stop people from creating a big tower to show how smart and important they were. God made us smart, and he likes it when we use our brains to do good things. But God wants us to thank him and praise him for the good things we can do. Let's thank God right now.

Thank you, God, for making me smart. *(Point to your head.)*

Help me to love you with all my heart! *(Point to your heart.)*

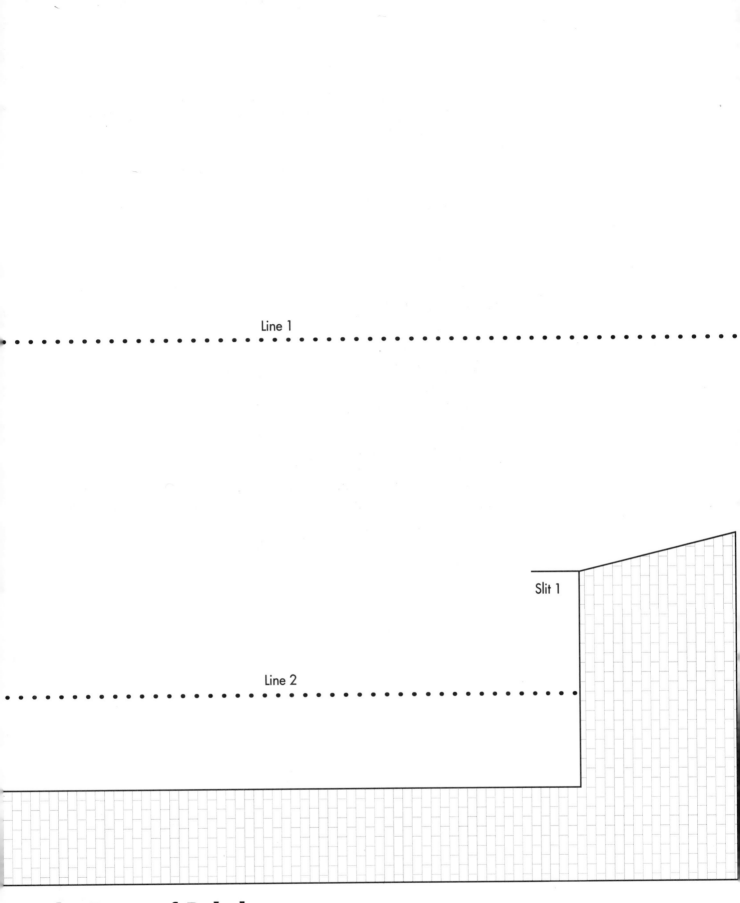

Line 1

Slit 1

Line 2

The Tower of Babel
Figure 1

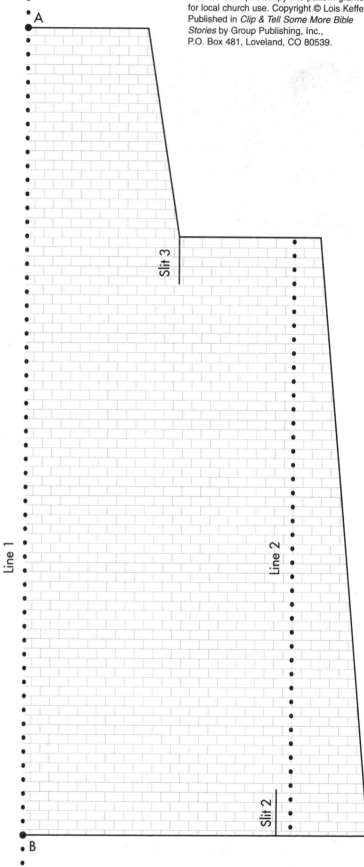

The Tower of Babel
Figure 2

A

Slit 3

Line 1

Line 2

Slit 2

B

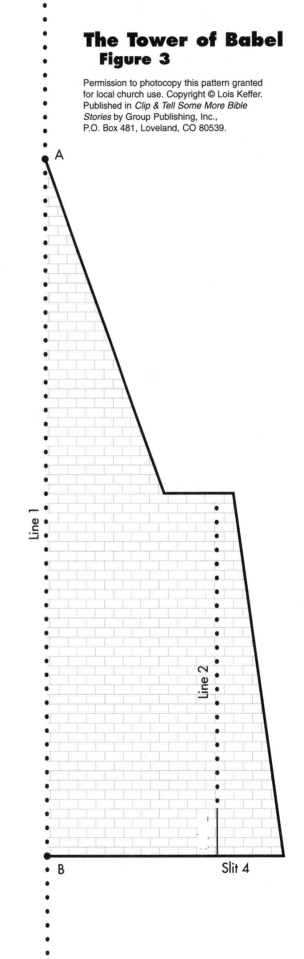

The Tower of Babel
Figure 3

A

Line 1

Line 2

B

Slit 4

GOD'S PROMISE TO ABRAHAM

PREPARATION

Copy Figure 1 (the circle of stars) onto shiny silver wrapping paper. Copy Figure 2 (the baby) onto beige paper. You'll also need an 8½x11 sheet of colored paper. The patterns for this story are on pages 20 and 21.

THE STORY

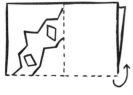

△ *Fold the silver paper in half on Line 1. Fold again on Line 2.*

Once, long ago, there lived a man named Abram. Abram loved and obeyed God, and God loved Abram.

✂ *Cut from A to B.*

God had special plans for Abram. God decided that Abram's family would become a nation of special people. But Abram was very old, and he didn't have any children.

✂ *Cut across the tops of the stars from C to D.*

"How can I be the father of a great nation if I have no children?" Abram wondered.

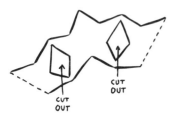

✂ *Cut away the spaces between the stars, being careful not to cut the stars apart at the bottom or the top.*

Then one night, God told Abram to go outside. "Look up at the sky," God said. "There are so many stars, you cannot count them."

☞ *Gently open the circle of stars.*

"Your family will be just like the stars. There will be too many to count!" God told Abram. Abram believed God. But a long time passed, and still Abram had no children.

☞ *Set Figure 1 aside. Place the colored paper underneath the beige paper, and fold both sheets in half on Line 1.*

Then one night, God spoke to Abram and said, "I am changing your name from Abram to Abraham because I am making you a father of many nations."

✂ *Cut around Figure 2 (the baby) from A to B.*

Even though Abraham was ninety-nine years old, he believed God's promise.

18

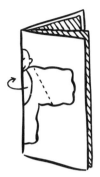

△ *Fold up on Line 2, revealing the colored "blanket."*

Not long after that, Abraham's wife became pregnant and had a son.

△ *Fold in on Lines 3 and 4, and display the baby.*

It was a miracle! Only God could make an old, old lady and an old, old man have a baby. And sure enough, a great nation grew from Abraham's son. God kept his promise to Abraham, and God will keep his promises to you, too!

You may want to have children cut and fold babies of their own. Teach this song to the tune of "The Mulberry Bush." Have children rock their babies as they sing.

Abraham had a baby boy,
A baby boy, a baby boy.
Abraham had a baby boy,
His father's pride and joy.

God did what he said he'd do,
Said he'd do, said he'd do.
God did what he said he'd do.
God's promises are true!

God's Promise to Abraham
Figure 1

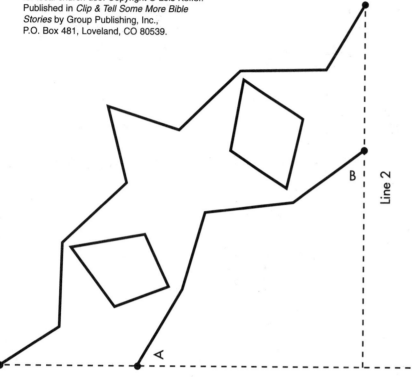

Line 1

Line 2

A

B

C

D

20

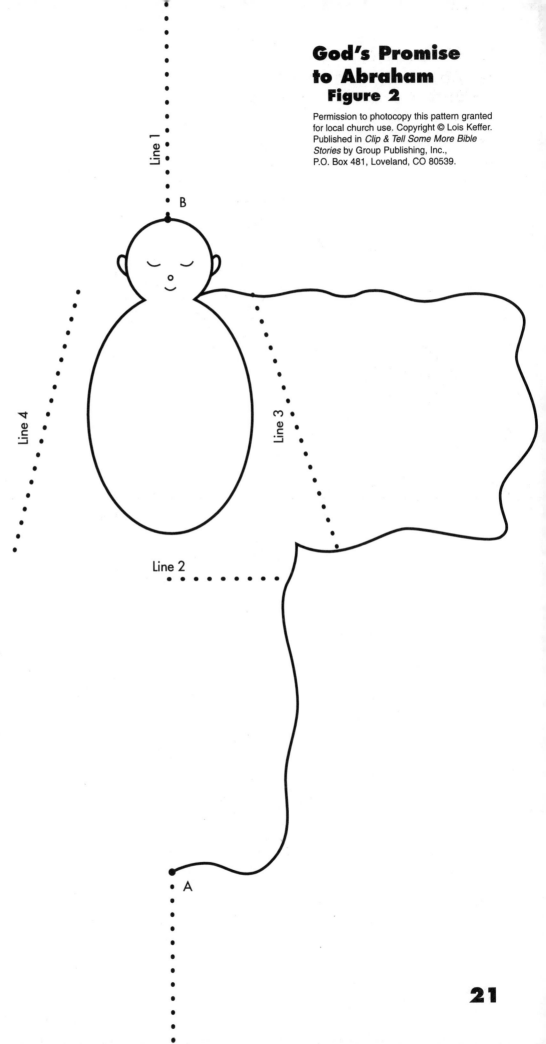

God's Promise to Abraham
Figure 2

Line 1

B

Line 4

Line 3

Line 2

A

AN ANGEL HELPS HAGAR

PREPARATION

Copy Figure 1 (Ishmael teasing) and Figure 2 (the water flask) onto brown paper. Copy Figure 3 (the angel and the stream of water) onto light-blue paper. The patterns for this story are on pages 24-26.

To bring the story to life for the children, you may want to let them prepare and eat a "thirsty" snack, such as soda crackers and peanut butter, just before you tell the story. Have cups and a pitcher of cool water or juice close by, but don't let anyone take a drink until the point in the story where God shows Hagar a well in the desert.

THE STORY

Abraham loved God more than anything. And he loved his two sons, Ishmael and Isaac. Ishmael was a teenager. His mother was the slave woman, Hagar. Isaac, the younger son, was only about three years old. Isaac's mother was Sarah, Abraham's wife.

Fold Figure 1 in half on Line 1.

God blessed Abraham and made him very rich. Someday all of Abraham's money and possessions would go to Isaac, because his mother was Abraham's wife.

Cut around the figure from A to B.

But since Ishmael's mother was just a slave, Ishmael wouldn't get much at all. That made Ishmael jealous.

Cut from C to D.

He thought little Isaac was spoiled.

So Ishmael teased Isaac and made fun of him.

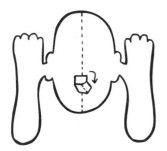

Open Figure 1 and fold forward on Line 2 so the boy's tongue is sticking out.

"Na-na na-na-na-na," Ishmael would say. "Isaac is a baby stuck in the gravy."

Did you ever have your feelings hurt when someone was teasing you? What was that like?

Set Figure 1 aside.

One day, Sarah saw Ishmael teasing Isaac. She grew furious and went rushing off to find Abraham.

Begin cutting around Figure 2.

"You must get rid of that slave woman and her son!" she demanded. "Ishmael must never get even a little bit of Isaac's inheritance!"

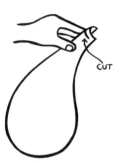

Abraham didn't know what to do. He loved both of his sons. Then God spoke to Abraham and said, "Don't worry about Hagar and Ishmael. Do what Sarah says."

👉 *Pinch the neck of the flask and cut Slit 1.*

Abraham always obeyed God, so the next morning he gave Hagar and Ishmael some food and a flask of water and sent them on their way. They walked into the desert, not knowing where to go or what to do. The hot sun beat down on their heads, and the burning sand hurt their feet. They took little sips of water from the flask, trying to make it last a long time.

👉 *Pretend to drink from the flask.*

But before long, the water was gone.

👉 *Set the flask aside.*

Hagar didn't know what to do.

✂ *Begin cutting around Figure 3.*

She told Ishmael to sit in the shade of a bush. Then she walked away, crying. "I cannot sit here and watch my son die," she thought. Alone in the desert, Hagar sobbed.

All at once, Hagar heard someone calling to her.

👉 *Display the angel.*

It was an angel! "What's the matter?" the angel asked. "Don't be afraid. God has heard the boy crying. Help him get up. God will make him the father of a great nation."

✂ *Cut from A to B to create a "stream of water."*

Then God showed Hagar a well of water, right in the middle of the desert!

👉 *Place the stream of water behind the flask, and push the tip of it through the slit in the flask.*

Hagar took Ishmael to the well, and both of them drank the cool, refreshing water.

👉 *Gently pull the stream of water through the slit in the flask. If you have a drink for the children, give it to them now.*

That day, Hagar and Ishmael learned that God takes care of us even when things look very bad.

Sure enough, Ishmael grew to be a strong, proud man who had twelve sons and a daughter.

An Angel Helps Hagar
Figure 1

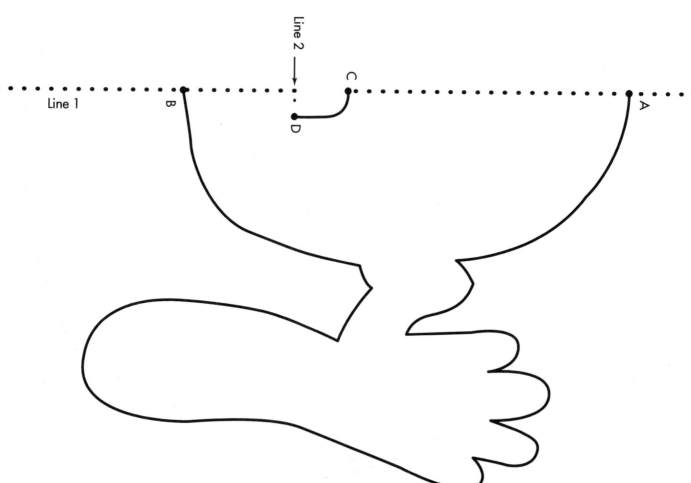

Line 2

Line 1

B

C

D

A

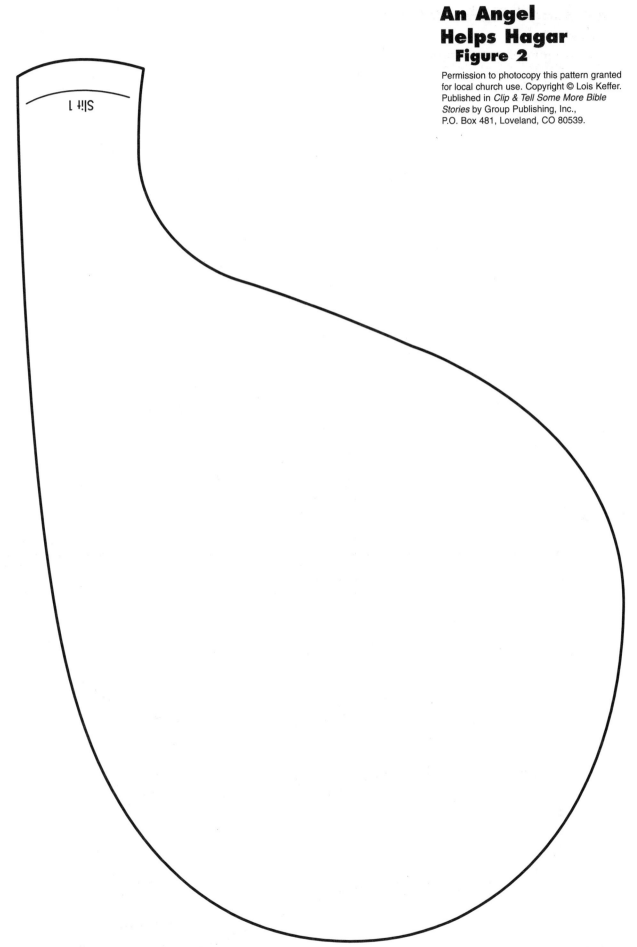

Slit 1

25

An Angel Helps Hagar
Figure 3

JACOB AND ESAU

PREPARATION

Copy Figure 1 (the twins) onto beige paper. Copy Figure 2 (the bowl of stew) onto red paper. The patterns for this story are on pages 29 and 30.

To bring this story alive for the children, bake a fragrant snack such as cinnamon rolls or cookies from refrigerated dough. Before the story, let children sniff the snack. Then explain that they'll have to be content with just smelling the snack right now, because you're not going to serve it until the end of the story.

THE STORY

Fold Figure 1 in half on Line 1.

Long ago, a woman named Rebekah had twins.

Cut around Figure 1, being sure the twins remain attached at the hand on the fold line.

The twins were boys.

Unfold Figure 1.

Esau was the older twin.

Make one of the twins "bow."

He had bushy red hair.

The younger twin was Jacob.

Make the other twin bow.

Jacob had smooth skin and dark hair.

The twins were different in other ways, too. Esau grew up to be a mighty hunter. He loved to be out in the fields. The twins' father, Isaac, was especially proud of Esau.

Make the first twin bow again.

Jacob preferred to stay among the tents and do quiet things. Rebekah was especially proud of Jacob.

Make the second twin bow again.

Because Esau had been born first, he would get most of the family's riches when his father died. Jacob and Rebekah didn't like that. They both wanted Jacob to get the most money and possessions.

Set the twins aside. Begin cutting around Figure 2.

One day when Esau came back from hunting, he found Jacob making

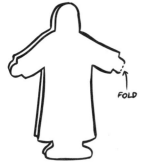

27

a pot of stew. Esau was starving, and the stew smelled wonderful.

☞ *Display the bowl of stew, and pretend to sniff the "steam" rising from it.*

What's it like to smell something wonderful when you're really, really hungry?

☞ *If you made a fragrant snack, let kids smell it once again.*

That's just how Esau felt. "Give me some of that stew," Esau said. "I'm starving!"

Jacob could see how much Esau wanted the stew. So he said, "I'll give you my stew if you'll give me your rights as the firstborn son."

Esau answered, "You can have my share of the money! Just give me that stew!"

Jacob gave him the stew. Jacob knew it was mean to trade stew for something so valuable as Esau's share of the family money. But he did it anyway.

☞ *Set the bowl of stew aside, and display the twins again.*

Later, Jacob did something else that was even meaner. When the twins' father, Isaac, was old and blind and about to die, Jacob pretended to be Esau. Isaac couldn't see very well, and he didn't know that Jacob was tricking him. So he gave Jacob a special blessing that should have gone to Esau. When Esau found out, he threatened to kill Jacob.

☞ *Turn the twins away from each other, back-to-back.*

So Jacob had to run away and live in another country. Many, many years passed before Jacob could come home again. He never got to see his mother or father again. Finally Jacob decided to come home. He didn't know if Esau was still angry or if Esau would try to kill him.

Esau rode out to meet Jacob and brought four hundred men with him. Jacob was scared. He couldn't possibly win against so many men! But Jacob walked up to meet his brother and bowed down low before him. Jacob felt bad about the mean tricks he'd played on Esau so many years before.

What do you think happened when the two brothers met?

☞ *Bend the outside arm of each twin forward and then fold the figures toward each other so they "hug."*

Esau ran up and gave Jacob a big hug. He forgave Jacob and invited him to live in that land with him.

☞ *If you prepared treats, serve them to the children now.*

Have you ever been mean to anyone in your family? I have. Sometimes we're mean to the people we love the most. But God wants us to be loving and kind and to forgive each other. Let's pray for God to help us do that.

Dear Lord, thank you for giving us families. Help us not to be mean like Jacob was. Help us to be loving and kind and forgiving. In Jesus' name, amen.

Line 1

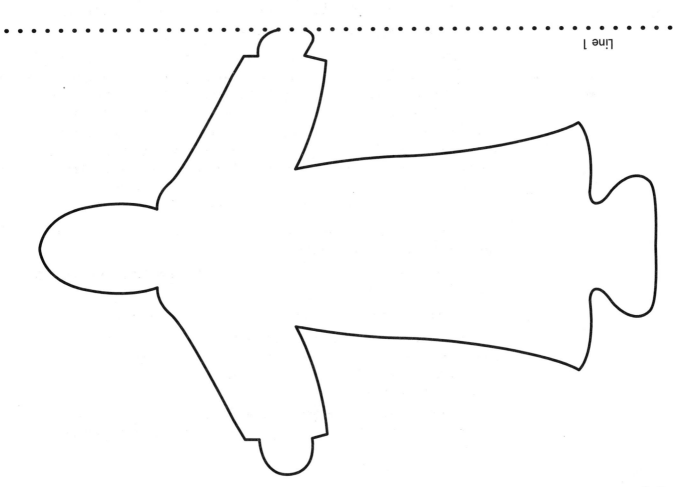

Jacob and Esau
Figure 2

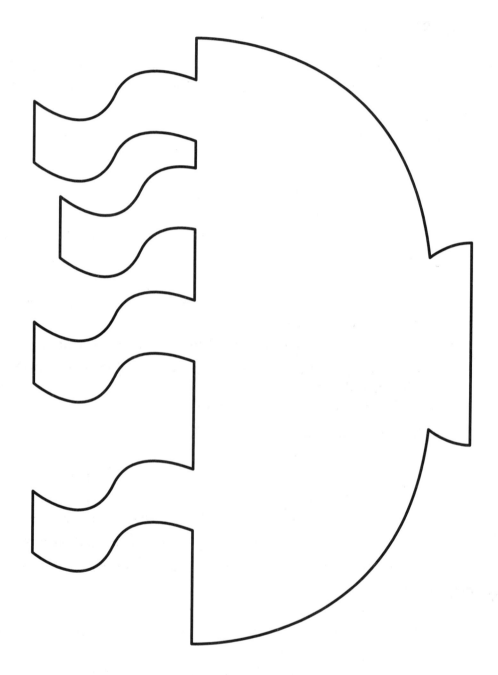

A PRINCESS FINDS A BABY

Copy Figure 1 (the palace) onto white paper. Copy Figure 2 (the basket in the grasses) onto green paper. The patterns for this story are on pages 33 and 34.

THE STORY

Once upon a time, there was a lovely princess who lived in a beautiful palace.

Fold Figure 1 in half on Line 1.

It sounds like I'm going to tell a fairy tale, doesn't it? But this is a true story from God's Word.

Cut around the figure from A to B, and open the palace.

The princess's father also lived in the palace. He was a mean king. He made a rule that all the boy babies born to God's people had to be killed. That made the kind princess sad.

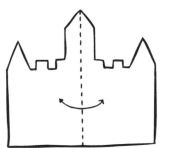

Set the palace aside. Cut Figure 2 from A to B.

The princess wasn't mean like her father.

Fold the basket up on Line 1. Then fold the figure in on Lines 2 and 3 to hide the basket.

One day the princess went down to the river to take a bath.

Cut from C to D, making sure to cut through all three layers.

Tall grasses grew by the riverside where the princess went for her bath.

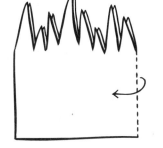

Open Figure 2 on Lines 2 and 3.

"Look!" the princess cried as she waded into the river. "There's a basket floating in the grasses!"

Fold the basket forward on Line 1 so children can see it.

She sent one of her servants to bring the basket to her. When the princess looked in the basket, she saw a baby boy. He was crying, and the kind princess felt sorry for him.

"This baby must be an Israelite," she said.

Suddenly a little girl ran up and asked, "Princess, would you like me to find someone to take care of the baby for you?"

"Yes!" answered the kind princess.

The princess didn't know it, but the little girl was the baby's sister. And the woman the girl brought to take care of the child was his own mother.

"Take care of this baby boy for me," the princess said, "and I will pay you. Then, when he's older, he can come to the palace and live with me."

That little baby boy grew up to be Moses, the mighty leader of God's people who helped them escape from the mean king. Just by being kind to a little tiny baby, the princess played an important part in God's plan.

Someday God may use you in a special way, just as he used the kind princess. Let's learn a song about that!

Teach this song to the tune of "Did You Ever See a Lassie?"
Oh, the princess saved a baby

(make a "crown" with your hands and then rock a pretend baby),
A baby, a baby.

(Rock a pretend baby.)
Oh, the princess saved a baby

(make a crown with your hands)
Who grew to serve God.

(Flex your muscles.)
So be kind when you can

(cross your hands over your heart and then point to someone),
For you're part of God's plan.

(Point to someone else and then point to heaven.)
Oh, the princess saved a baby

(make a crown with your hands)
Who grew to serve God.

(Flex your muscles.)

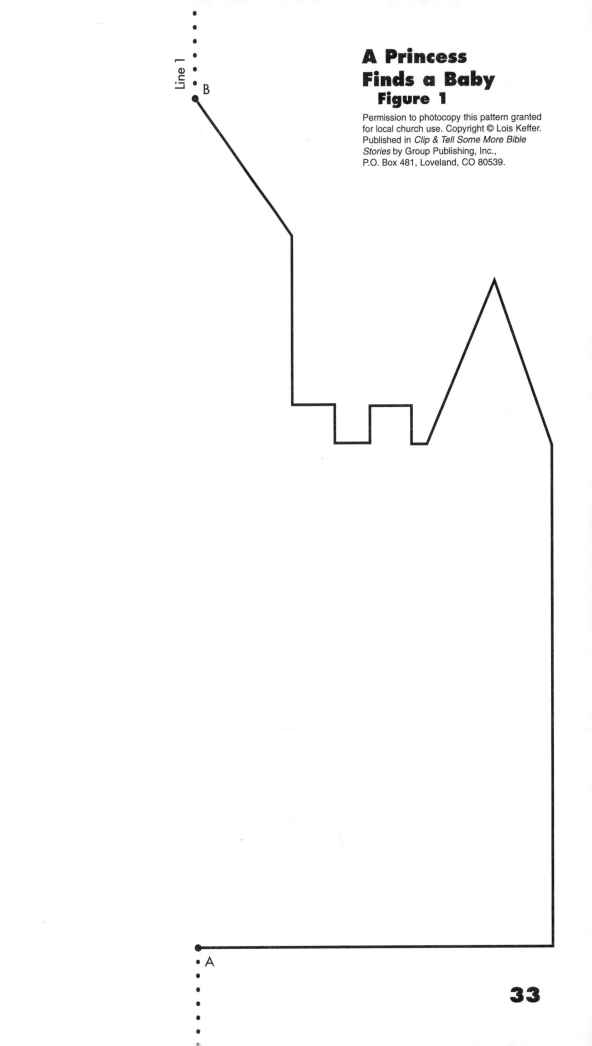

Line 1

B

A Princess
Finds a Baby
Figure 1

A

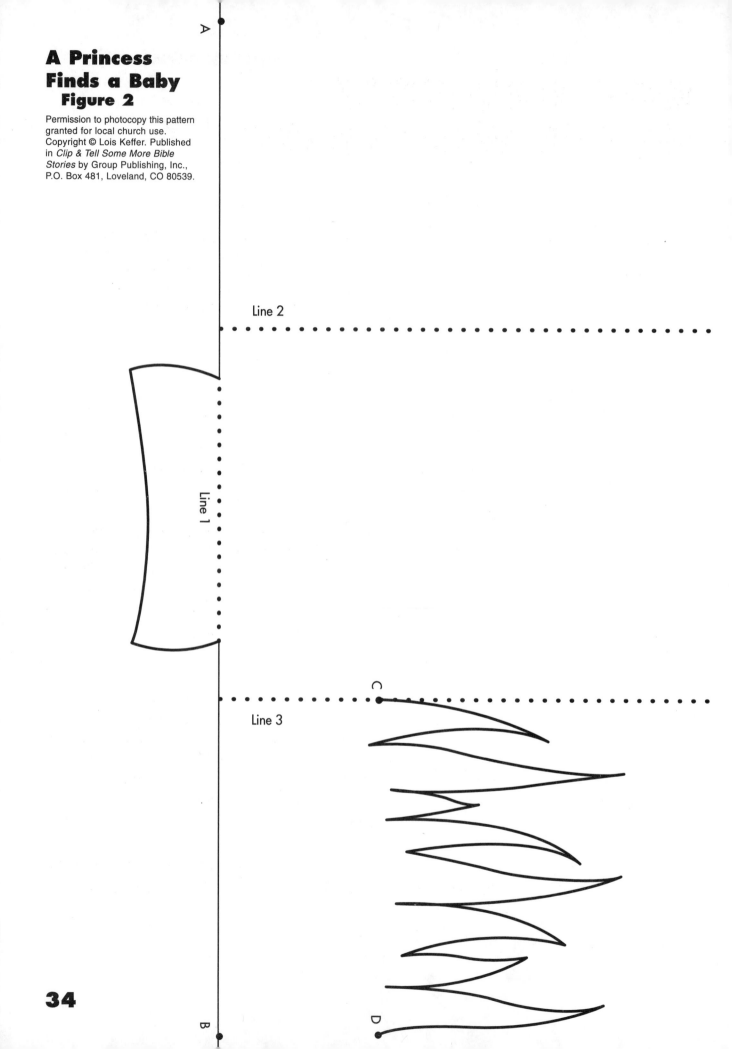

A Princess Finds a Baby
Figure 2

A

Line 2

Line 1

Line 3

C

D

34

B

GOD PROVIDES IN THE WILDERNESS

PREPARATION

Copy Figure 1 (the quail) onto tan paper. Figure 2 (the basket) is a simple origami box folded from an 8½x11 sheet of paper. Photocopy the instructions, or simply lay the open book in your lap. The numbers by the instructions in the story correspond with the numbered steps in the pattern. The patterns for this story are on pages 37 and 38.

THE STORY

For many years, God's people lived in Egypt as slaves of a mean king. They had to work hard day and night. When they cried out to God for help, God sent Moses to be their leader. God helped Moses perform great miracles, and finally the king of Egypt let God's people go.

Fold Figure 1 in half on Line 1. Cut around the figure from A to B and then open it.

Hundreds of thousands of God's people followed Moses into the wilderness on their way to the Promised Land. That was a lot of people to feed! After just a few days, the food they had brought with them ran out.

Turn the paper over, and fold the corners into the center on Lines 2 and 3.

Their empty tummies grumbled, and they began to mumble!

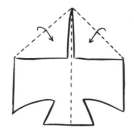

Fold back on Line 1.

"You should've left us in Egypt, Moses!" they complained. "At least there we had plenty to eat. Did you bring us out here to die?"

Then God told Moses, "I've heard my people grumbling. Speak to the people and tell them that I will rain down food from the sky. In the evening they will eat meat. And in the morning they'll have bread—all they want! Then they will know that I am the Lord their God."

To spread the wings, fold forward on Lines 4 and 5.

Sure enough, right about supper time, huge flocks of quails flew into the camp.

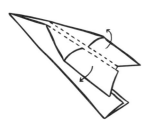

"Fly" the bird to a child and then have him or her fly it back to you.

That night, everyone enjoyed a delicious meal of freshly roasted quail. Mmm!

Set the quail aside.

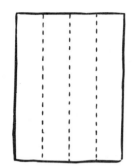

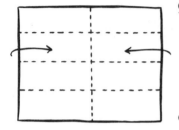

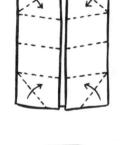

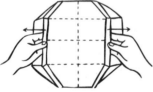

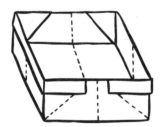

1. Fold a sheet of 8½x11-inch paper in half the long way, then open it. Fold the two edges to the center, then open it.

And the next morning, there was another surprise!

2. Fold the paper in half the other way, then open it. Fold the two edges to the center.

The ground all around the camp glistened with dew.

3. Fold each of the four corners in to the first folded line.

When the dew dried up, thin, frosty-looking flakes covered the ground.

4. Fold the middle strips back.

"What is it?" the people asked.

"This is bread from the Lord," Moses answered.

5, 6. Gently pull back on the middle edges until they become the outside edges of the box.

So the people took baskets and gathered up all the bread they needed.

Pretend to pick up manna and place it in the basket.

They called God's special bread "manna," which is Hebrew for "What is it?" Every morning God sent manna, and every evening God sent flocks of quails. God's people never went hungry again during all the many years they traveled in the desert.

You may want to let children make their own quails and manna baskets. Let them fly the quails and use the baskets to gather popcorn flying out of a popcorn popper without a lid!

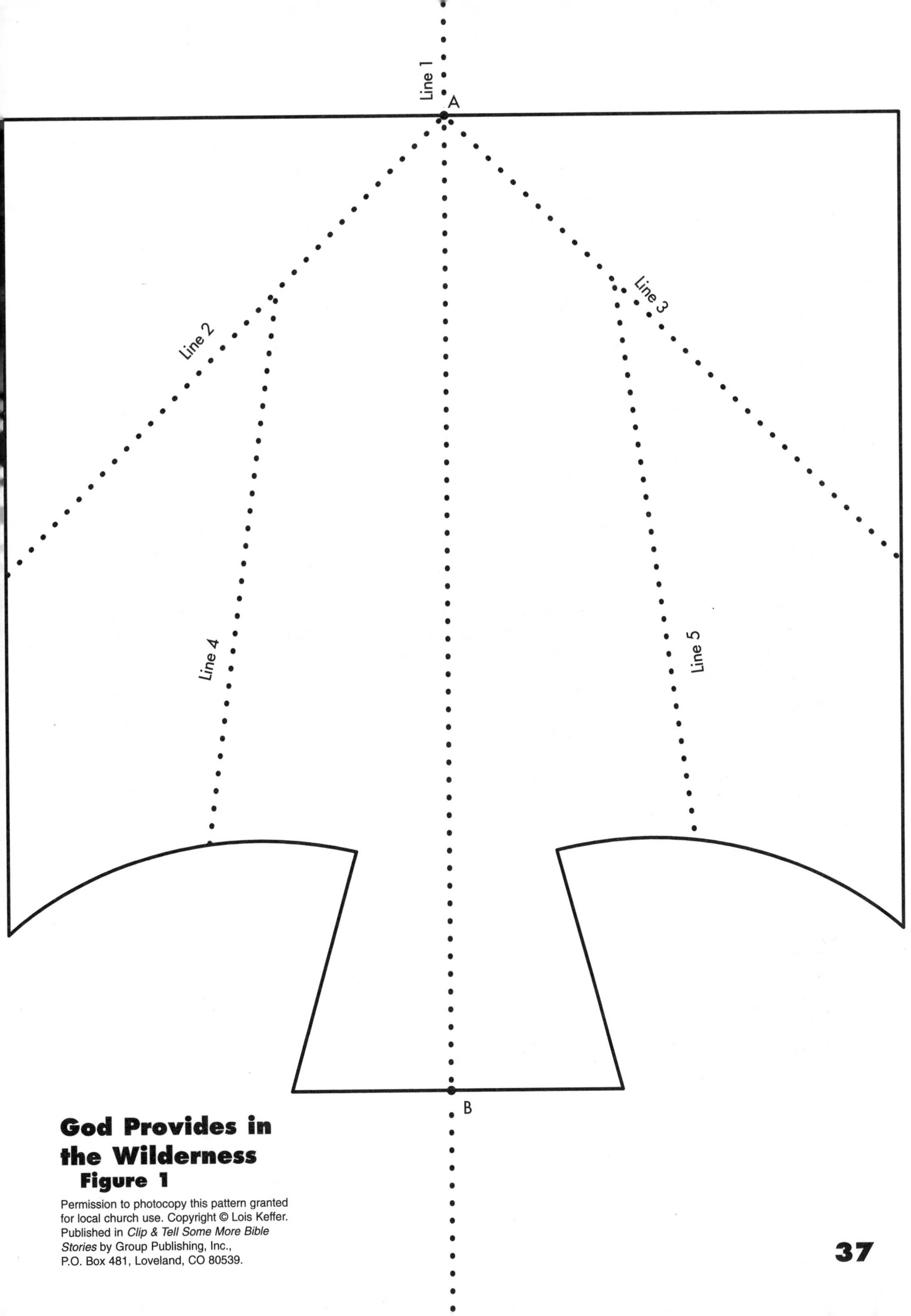

Line 1

A

Line 2

Line 3

Line 4

Line 5

B

God Provides in
the Wilderness
Figure 1

Permission to photocopy this pattern granted
for local church use. Copyright © Lois Keffer.
Published in *Clip & Tell Some More Bible
Stories* by Group Publishing, Inc.,
P.O. Box 481, Loveland, CO 80539.

37

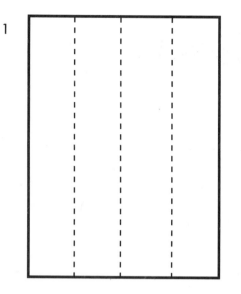

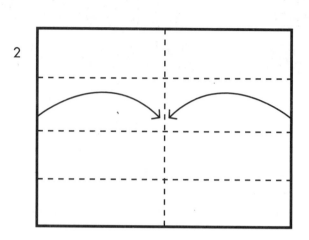

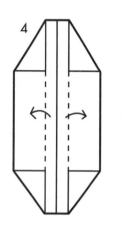

God Provides in the Wilderness
Figure 2

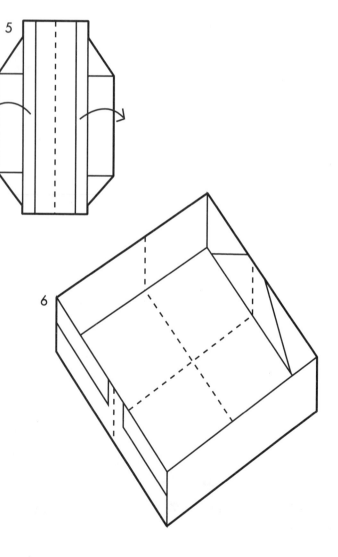

GOD GIVES THE TEN COMMANDMENTS

PREPARATION

Copy Figure 1 (the mountain) onto dark brown paper. Copy Figure 2 (the smoke) onto black paper. Copy Figure 3 (the fire) onto red or orange paper. Make copies of Figure 4 (the Ten Commandments) on white paper. You'll need one copy of Figure 4 for each child in the group. The patterns for this story are on pages 41-44.

THE STORY

God loved his special people, the Israelites, very much. God showed how much he loved his people by doing great miracles to help them escape from Egypt and by sending them food as they traveled through the wilderness. Then God showed how much loved his people by doing one more wonderful thing—God gave them special rules to teach them how to live.

Do you think rules are wonderful? Not everyone does! But just think of all the terrible things that could happen if we didn't have rules. People would be fighting and stealing and lying and hurting each other all the time. It would be awful! And God didn't want his people to have an awful time.

So after the Israelites had been traveling in the wilderness for three months, God led them to set up camp in front of Mount Sinai.

✂ *Cut out Figure 1.*

God called Moses to climb partway up the mountain, and there God spoke to Moses.

"Tell my people this," God said. "You saw all the things I did to bring you out of Egypt. I carried you like an eagle carries her young, and I brought you here to me. I have chosen you to be my special people."

Moses climbed back down the mountain and told these things to the people.

"We will obey God and do everything he has said," they promised.

✂ *Cut out Figure 2.*

Moses climbed back up the mountain. Then God said, "Tell the people to prepare themselves. I will come down the mountain, and they will see me. But they must not come near the mountain."

So the people washed their clothes and got ready to meet God.

☞ *Place Figure 2 behind Figure 1 so the smoke appears on top of the mountain.*

As they gathered in front of the mountain, a thick cloud of smoke gathered over the mountaintop.

✂ *Cut out Figure 3. Place Figure 3 between Figures 1 and 2 so the fire appears between the mountaintop and the smoke.*

The people could see flashes of fire and lightning. The whole mountain shook, and the ground trembled!

As the people listened, God gave Moses ten important laws. We call those laws the Ten Commandments.

God said, "I am the Lord your God; don't worship anyone else.

Don't make idols.

Be careful how you use my name.

Honor the Sabbath day by resting and worshiping me.

Honor your father and mother.

Don't murder.

Don't wish for someone else's husband or wife.

Don't steal.

Don't tell lies.

And don't want things that belong to other people."

God knew that if his people lived by those rules, they would be safe and happy.

God carved those rules into stone tablets so Moses could take them to the people. Let's have fun learning a rhyme that will help us remember God's Ten Commandments.

👉 *If your children can read, hand out Figure 4 (the stone tablets). If your children are nonreaders, teach the rhyme by having them repeat each line after you. Then hand out the stone tablets for children to take home.*

God Gives the
Ten Commandments
Figure 1

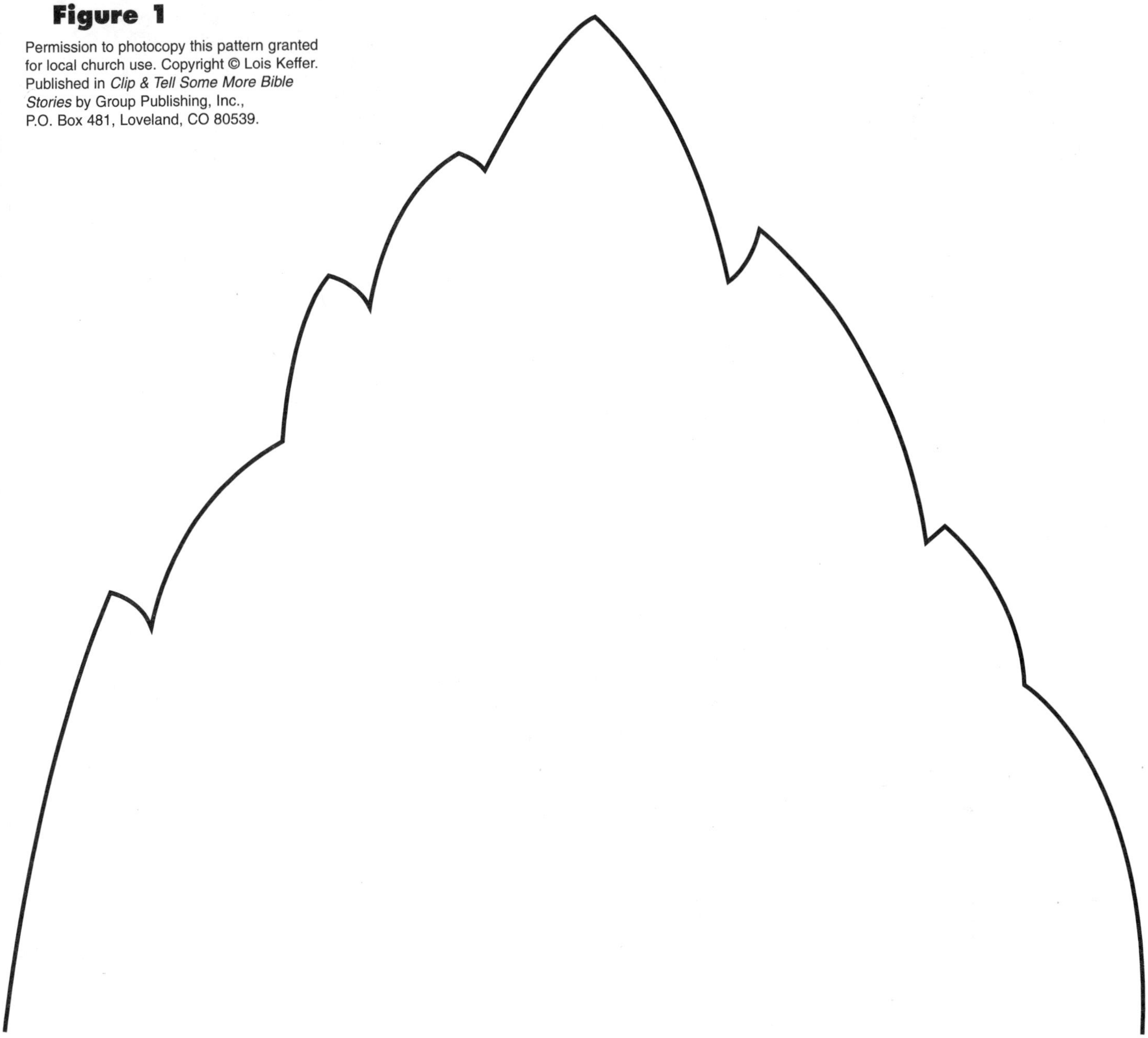

God Gives the
Ten Commandments
Figure 3

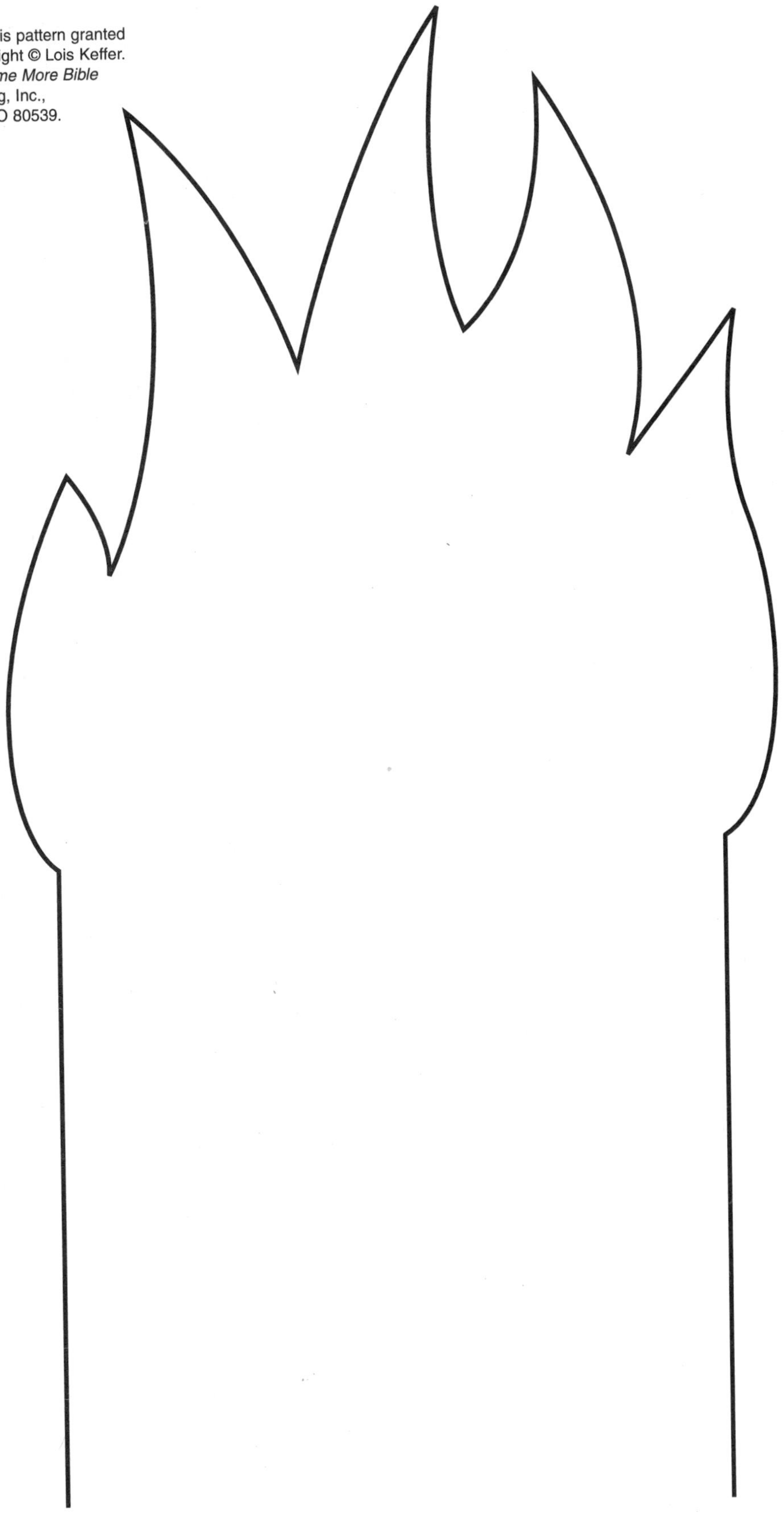

God Gives the Ten Commandments
Figure 4

Permission to photocopy this pattern granted for local church use. Copyright © Lois Keffer. Published in *Clip & Tell Some More Bible Stories* by Group Publishing, Inc., P.O. Box 481, Loveland, CO 80539.

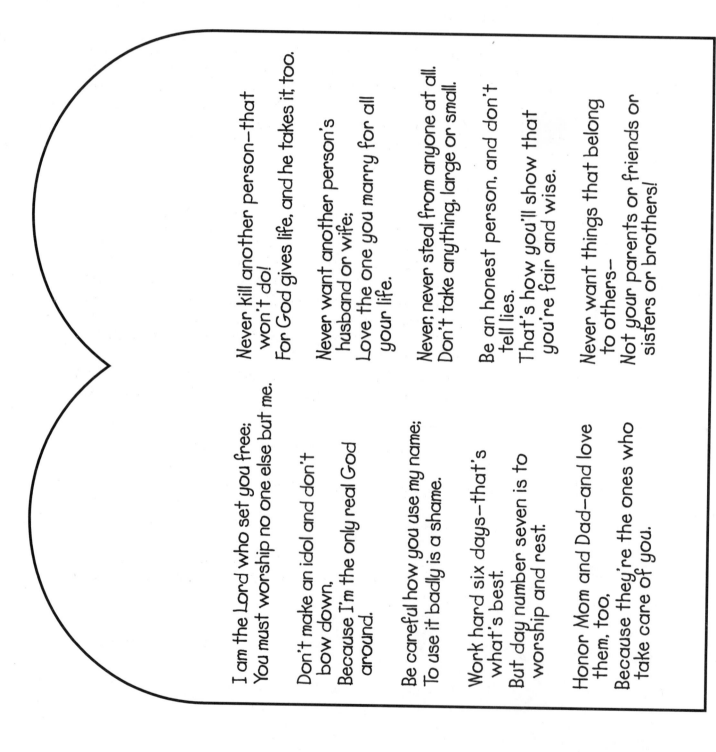

I am the Lord who set you free;
You must worship no one else but me.

Don't make an idol and don't bow down,
Because I'm the only real God around.

Be careful how you use my name;
To use it badly is a shame.

Work hard six days—that's what's best.
But day number seven is to worship and rest.

Honor Mom and Dad—and love them, too,
Because they're the ones who take care of you.

Never kill another person—that won't do!
For God gives life, and he takes it, too.

Never want another person's husband or wife;
Love the one you marry for all your life.

Never, never steal from anyone at all.
Don't take anything, large or small.

Be an honest person, and don't tell lies.
That's how you'll show that you're fair and wise.

Never want things that belong to others—
Not your parents or friends or sisters or brothers!

OFFERINGS FOR THE TABERNACLE

PREPARATION

Copy Figures 1-6 (the bracelet, the earring, the ring, the jar, the ark of the covenant, and the lamp stand) onto shiny gold paper. Copy Figure 7 (the offering box) onto colorful card stock. You'll need one copy of the offering box for each child. Before the story, use a craft knife to open the slits on the offering boxes.

The patterns for this story are on pages 47-50.

THE STORY

When God's people, the Israelites, were camped in front of Mount Sinai, God came down the mountain and talked to Moses there. But God didn't plan for the Israelites to stay at Mount Sinai. God promised to lead the people to a land of their own—a land where they would be free.

But God wanted to continue to meet with the people as he had at Mount Sinai. So God spoke to Moses about building a tabernacle where God would meet with the people and where they could worship God and give their offerings and sacrifices.

Of course, since they were traveling, they couldn't build a building like our church! But they could build a tent, and that's just what God wanted them to do.

God told Moses to ask the people to give offerings to help build the tabernacle. They would need goatskins and beautiful purple cloth for the tent itself and the curtains that would hang inside to make different rooms. They would need gold and silver and bronze to make the altar and the lamp stands and all the different items to furnish the tabernacle. They would need fabric and jewels and yarn and thread to make clothes for the priests.

So Moses gathered the Israelites and said, "The Lord has told me to take an offering so that we can build a tabernacle. If you are willing, please bring an offering."

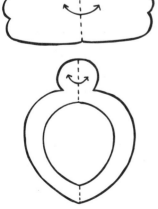

△ *Fold Figures 1-4 in half on Line 1.*

So all the people went back to their own tents and decided what to give as their offerings.

✂ *Cut Figure 1 from A to B.*

They chose fine gold jewelry including bracelets,

✂ *Cut Figure 2 from C to D and then from E to F.*

earrings,

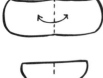

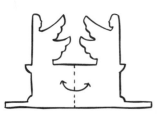

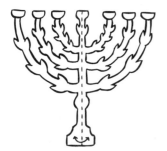

✂ *Cut Figure 3 from G to H.*

and rings.

✂ *Cut Figure 4 from I to J.*

And they chose jars of oil and perfume.

The next morning, the people brought their offerings to Moses. And they continued to bring offerings the morning after that, and the morning after that, until there was more than enough to make all the things needed for the tabernacle. Moses finally had to ask the people to stop bringing offerings! God was pleased that his people had given so generously.

Then the work on the tabernacle began. God chose two skilled craftsmen to organize the work and teach the helpers what to do.

◄ *Fold Figure 5 in half on Line 1.*

God gave instructions for building the ark of the covenant.

✂ *Cut Figure 5 from A to B.*

It was a special wooden chest made to hold the tablets with the Ten Commandments written on them. The chest was to be covered with pure gold inside and out, and two angels were to cover the top with their wings.

◄ *Fold Figure 6 in half on Line 1, and cut from A to B. You may simplify the figure by cutting off the leaves rather than cutting around them.*

God told Moses how to make all the other furnishings needed for the tabernacle. There were altars and bowls and tables and lamps and beautiful lamp stands.

So all the skilled craftsmen and craftswomen worked together to melt and mold, carve, and sew to make beautiful furnishings for the tabernacle just as God commanded. When everything was ready, Moses put up the beautiful tent and the courtyard around it and then put all the furnishings just where God wanted them. When everything was in place, God's glory appeared in a cloud, and it filled the tabernacle. Whenever the Israelites saw the cloud resting on the tabernacle, they remembered that God was with them.

Just as the Israelites brought offerings to build the tabernacle, we give offerings to help with God's work today.

Who knows how our offerings are used?

God gives so many good things to us, it's only natural to give something back. God likes it when we give with a cheerful heart. I have offering boxes for you to make. You can use them to bring your offerings to God.

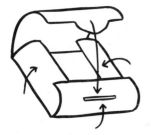

☞ *Pass out the offering box patterns (Figure 7). Help children cut on the solid lines and fold inward on the dotted lines. Show them how to push the pointed end through the slit on the other end to form a box with a curved top. The slit on the top is a coin slot.*

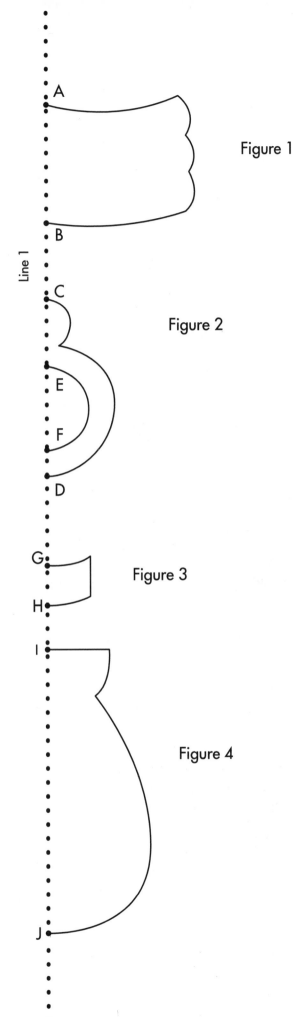

A

Figure 1

B

Line 1

C

Figure 2

E

F

D

G

Figure 3

H

I

Figure 4

J

Offerings for the Tabernacle
Figures 1-4

Offerings for the Tabernacle
Figure 5

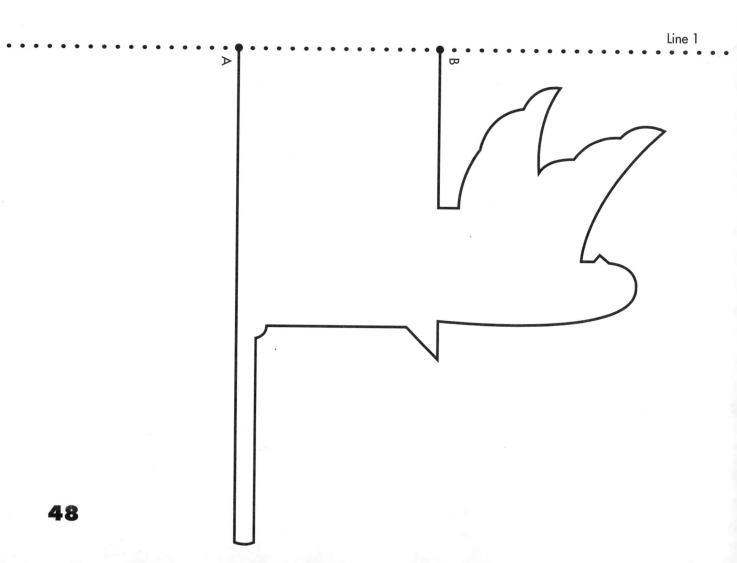

Line 1

A

B

B
Line 1
A

Offerings for
the Tabernacle
Figure 7

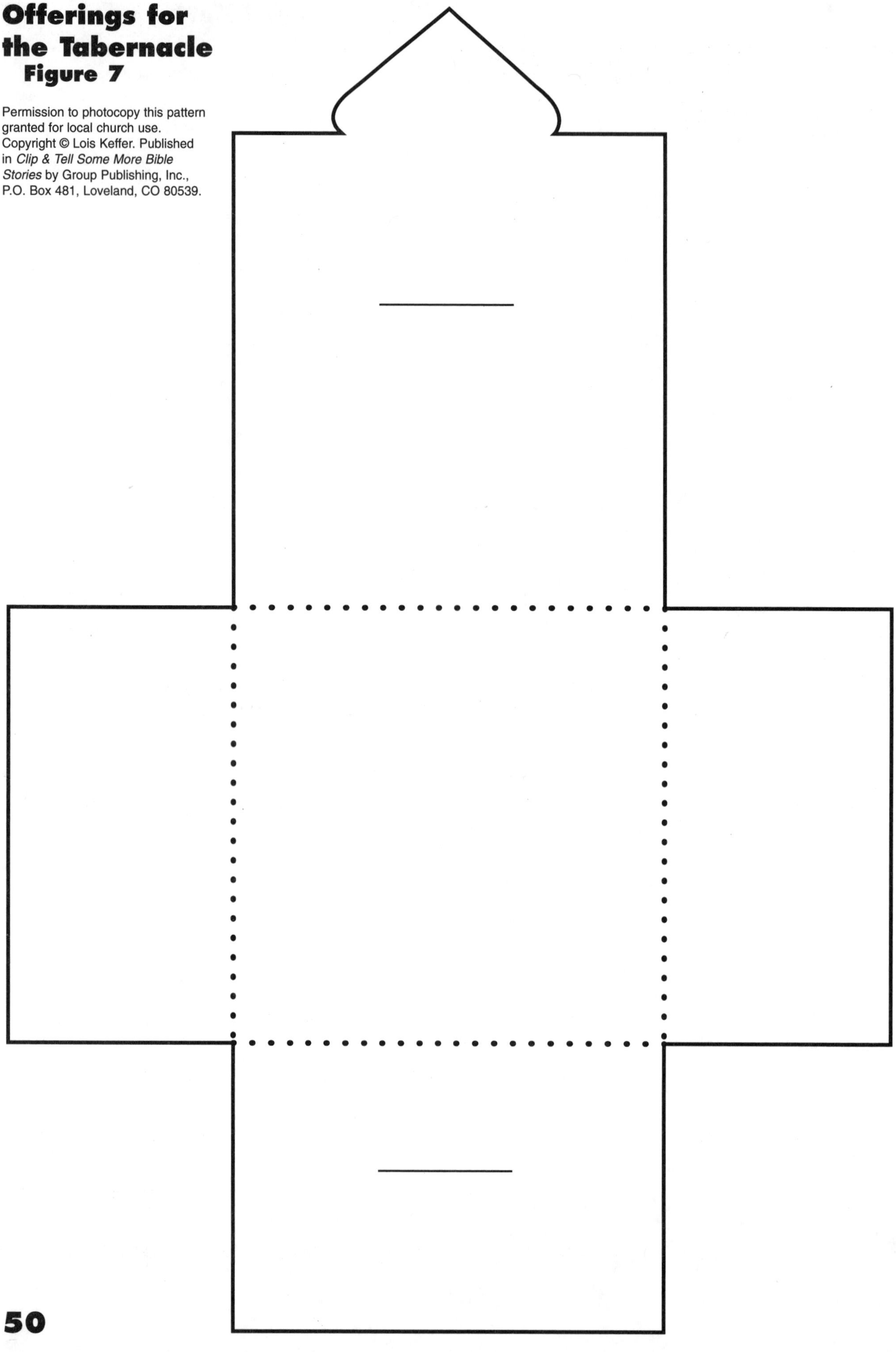

THE FEAST OF BOOTHS

PREPARATION

Make four copies of page 53. You'll need two copies on brown paper and two copies on green paper.

At the close of the story, you may want to serve the children treats such as the Jewish people might have enjoyed during the Feast of Booths.

THE STORY

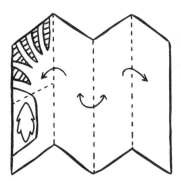

Harvest time was a happy time for God's people.

◭ *Take one of the brown sheets of paper. Fold Figure 1 up (a valley fold) on Line 1.*

Bringing in good crops meant that there would be plenty to eat over the long winter.

◭ *Fold down (mountain folds) on Lines 2 and 3.*

There would be grapes for raisins and for making wine, flour for making bread, and figs to dry into special sweet cakes.

✄ *Cut from A to B.*

God wanted the Israelites to remember that the good harvest came because of God's goodness. God provided the seeds and soil and sent the rain and the sunshine so the crops would grow.

✄ *Cut away the shaded areas between the branches.*

So God told the people to have a special celebration at harvest time.

◭ *Fold forward and back on Line 4.*

We have a special celebration at harvest time. Do you know what it is? That's right! It's Thanksgiving.

☜ *Open and flatten the fold on Line 1. Make corners at Lines 2 and 3, and stand the figure up.*

The Jewish celebration was called the Feast of Booths. I think you would like it!

☜ *Bend the branches forward on Line 4, creating a roof. You now have one-half of a booth.*

God said that all the families should build shelters from branches and leaves, kind of like the booth I'm making right now.

☜ *Follow the above steps with the second sheet of brown paper.*

Then everyone would camp out in the booths for a whole week! Some families made their booths on the roofs of their houses. Others made them in their courtyards or even in the street. It was a happy time of celebration that everyone looked forward to all year!

☞ *Place the two halves of the booth together.*

By camping out, the people would remember how God led the Israelites through the wilderness for forty years before they entered the Promised Land.

◺ *Accordion-fold the green paper on the dotted lines. Cut around each palm branch.*

They would remember how God took care of them during that long, long trip. And they would celebrate the fact that now they lived in the Promised Land and enjoyed God's blessing on their crops.

☞ *Lay the palm branches on top of the roof of the booth.*

During the week they made special sacrifices and offerings to God. They danced together and sang songs of thanksgiving. And on the last day, they listened to the leaders read God's law.

Now let's give thanks before we enjoy some of the Bible-time foods the Israelites enjoyed at their feast.

Let children sample raisins, shepherd's bread, fresh grape juice, and dried or canned figs. For even more fun, let the children build a booth of their own by draping a blanket over a table and spreading the top of the blanket with branches or green crepe paper streamers. Serve the treat inside the booth.

The Feast of Booths
Figures 1-2

Line 3

Line 1

Line 2

Line 4

B

A

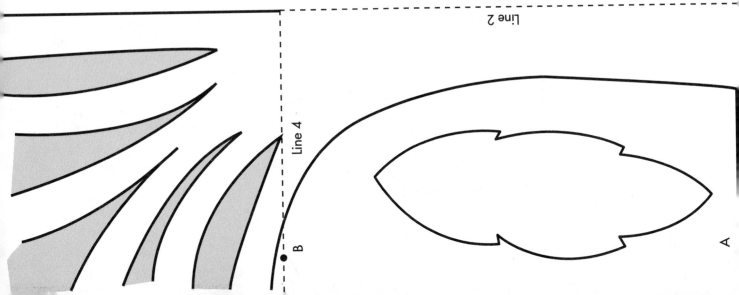

LOVE THE LORD WITH ALL YOUR HEART

PREPARATION

Copy Figure 1 (the heart) onto red paper. Copy Figure 2 (the phylactery) onto tan paper. You'll need one phylactery for each child. The patterns for this story are on pages 56 and 57.

Before the story, use a craft knife to open the slit on each phylactery. Prepare a sample phylactery to show the children. Cut on all the solid lines. Fold in on Lines 1 and 2 so the tab fits into the slit. Fold back on Lines 3, 4, 5, and 6 to form the straps. Bend the straps back behind the box containing the verse, and slide one strap inside the other. The straps are long enough to fit around an adult's wrist or a child's arm and should remain fairly secure without tape so the phylactery can be put on and removed.

THE STORY

On Figure 1, fold back (toward the blank side of the paper) on Lines 1 and 2.

Many books of the Bible tell us how God wants us to live.

Fold up on Line 3 (a valley fold).

The first five books of the Bible are called the books of the Law. Those books tell us about God's special people, the Israelites, and the rules God gave them to live by.

Cut from A to B.

Do you know what rule was most important to God?

Cut from C to D.

More than anything else, God wanted the Israelites to love him with all their hearts.

Open the heart so the words are facing you.

To help them remember to love God, the Israelites said this verse every day: "Hear, O Israel: The Lord our God, the Lord is one. Love the Lord your God with all your heart and with all your soul and with all your strength."

Fold the two heart halves back to cover the words.

This heart reminds us that the most important thing for us to do is to love God with our whole heart.

Turn the heart around and open the halves, revealing the words to the children.

God also told his people to teach their children about all the wonderful things God had done for them. Do you remember that God did great miracles to help his people escape from Egypt? Can anyone remember what some of those miracles were?

Do you remember how God fed his people and took care of them in the wilderness? Who can remember how God fed them?

Do you remember that God met Moses on a mountain and wrote the Ten Commandments on stone tablets? Who can tell me one of the Ten Commandments?

God wanted his people to tell their children about all these wonderful things. Then when those children grew up and became parents, they could tell their children, then those people could tell their children, and so on.

When you grow up, if you have children, what will you tell them about God?

Do you remember that verse that the Israelites repeated every day to help them remember that loving God was the most important thing of all? Back in Bible times, people used to carry that verse in a little leather box on their arms or on their foreheads. That little box was called a phylactery (fill-ACT-ur-ee).

Slip on the sample phylactery.

I have a phylactery for each of you to make!

Help children make phylacteries and put them on. Most children younger than six will need adult assistance.

Let's open our phylacteries and say the verse together. I'll say a line and you repeat it after me. Here we go!

"Hear, O Israel:

The Lord our God,

the Lord is one.

Love the Lord your God

with all your heart

and with all your soul

and with all your strength."

Good job!

How are you going to show that you love God today?

Let's pray. Dear Lord, we do love you with all our heart. Thank you for giving us your Word and teaching us how to live safe, happy lives. Help us remember that our number one job is to love you. In Jesus' name, amen.

Love the Lord
With All Your Heart
Figure 1

Line 2

Line 3

Line 1

Love the Lord With All Your Heart
Figure 2

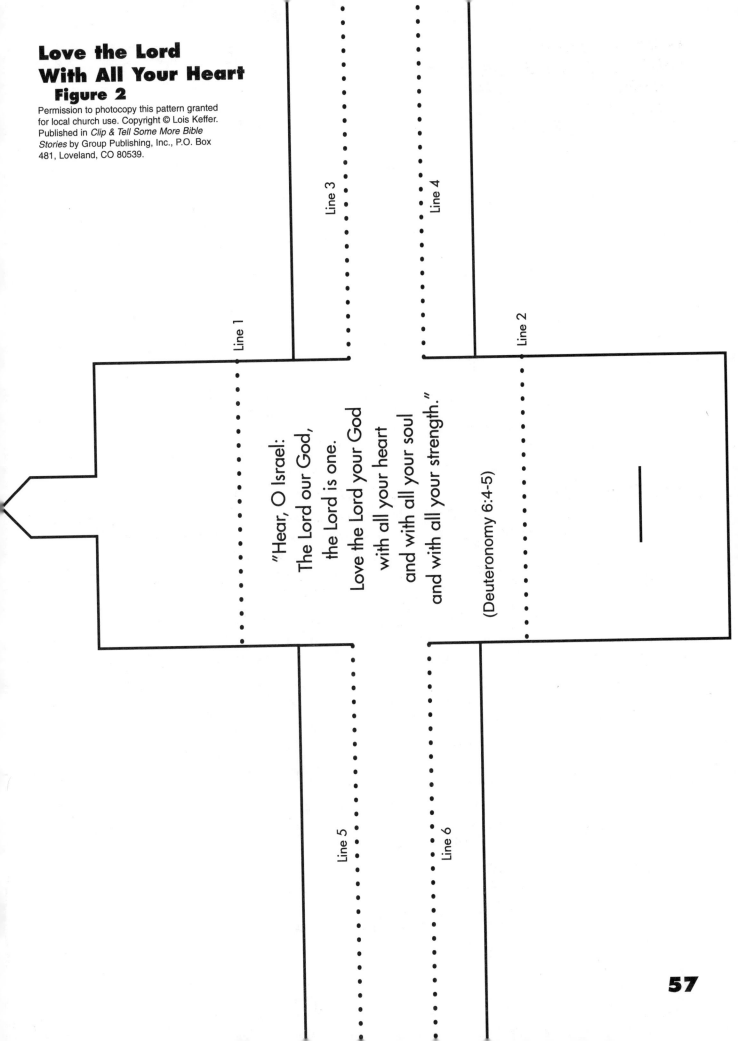

Line 3

Line 4

Line 1

Line 2

"Hear, O Israel:
The Lord our God,
the Lord is one.
Love the Lord your God
with all your heart
and with all your soul
and with all your strength."

(Deuteronomy 6:4-5)

Line 5

Line 6

GOD HELPS GIDEON

PREPARATION

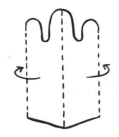

Copy Figure 1 (the shrinking army) onto tan paper. Copy Figures 2 and 3 (the flaming torch and the trumpet) onto gold paper. Copy Figure 4 (the clay jar) onto brown paper. The patterns for this story are on pages 60-62.

THE STORY

God's people were afraid. Their enemies, the Midianites, would bring a great army into Israel every year just when it was time to harvest the crops. The Midianites would steal all the crops and livestock, leaving the Israelites poor and hungry. Because there were so many of them, God's people couldn't protect themselves.

Fold Figure 1 in half on Line 1. Cut from A to B.

Finally the Israelites cried out to God for help, and God sent them a leader named Gideon. Gideon was hiding in a wine press. Gideon hoped he could thresh his wheat in the wine press without being seen by the Midianites. An angel came to Gideon and said, "Hail, mighty warrior!"

Gideon thought, "Who, me?"

Cut from B to C.

Gideon was just as afraid as everyone else was, but God wanted him to fight the Midianites. So Gideon gathered an army of 32,000 men.

Open Figure 1.

When God saw how many men Gideon had gathered, God said, "You have too many men. Tell them that anyone who is afraid may go home."

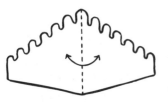

Fold back on Lines 2 and 3.

So 22,000 men went home. That left only 10,000 men to fight the Midianites.

Then God spoke to Gideon again. "You still have too many men. Take them to a stream to get a drink of water. Keep only those men who lap up the water like dogs. Send home anyone who kneels down to drink."

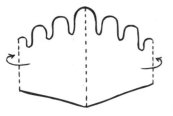

Fold back on Lines 4 and 5.

Only 300 men lapped the water like dogs! So 9,700 men went home, while only 300 stayed to fight the Midianites! But God knew what he was doing. God told Gideon to sneak down to the Midianite camp.

✂ *Cut Figures 2 and 3 apart on Line 1.*

Gideon could hear the Midianites talking about how scared they were of the Israelite army.

✂ *Cut out Figure 2 (the flaming torch), and lay it in your lap.*

Gideon knew God would help him.

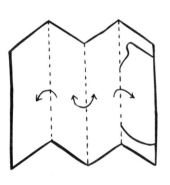

▱ *Fold Figure 3 on the dotted line, and cut out the trumpet.*

So Gideon began to prepare his men for battle.

▱ *Fold Figure 4 in half on Line 1, and cut the slit.*

Gideon gave his men the strangest weapons you've ever seen!

▱ *Fold Figure 4 up on Line 1 and back on Lines 2 and 3.*

If you were sending soldiers into battle, what weapons would you give them? Remember—they didn't have guns back then.

✂ *Cut from A to B and from C to D.*

Well, here's what Gideon gave his little army.

☞ *Hold up the trumpet and the clay jar.*

He gave them each a trumpet and a clay jar

☞ *Open the clay jar, and slide the handle of the torch into the slit.*

and a flaming torch to hide inside the jar. Then he had his army surround the Midianite camp late at night. At Gideon's signal, all the soldiers blew their trumpets, broke open their jars,

☞ *Open the jar.*

held up their torches, and cried as loud as they could, "A sword for the Lord and for Gideon!" Shout that with me as I hold up my torch. "A sword for the Lord and for Gideon!" The Midianites were caught by surprise. They were so terrified that they started fighting each other, and the Israelites chased them far across the border. After Gideon's great victory, the Midianites never bothered the Israelites again.

When something big and scary is happening to you, just remember Gideon and his tiny army. God helped Gideon, and God will help you, too!

Teach children this action rhyme by having them repeat each line after you.

Standin' in a wine press *(cross your hands over your heart),*
Shaking with fear *(shake all over),*
Hoping there's no enemy
Sneakin' around here. *(Tiptoe in place.)*
Look at all our enemies *(point)*
Shakin' with fear. *(Shake all over.)*
When this battle's over *(make fists),*
They'll know God was here! *(Shake your finger and point to the sky.)*

(poem excerpted from Sunday School Specials 3 by Lois Keffer)

God Helps Gideon
Figure 1

- -

Line 3

- -

Line 5

Line 1

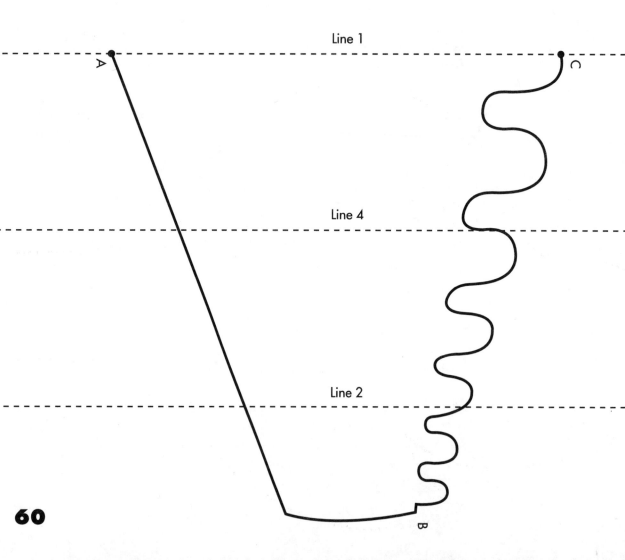

Line 4

Line 2

God Helps Gideon
Figures 2-3

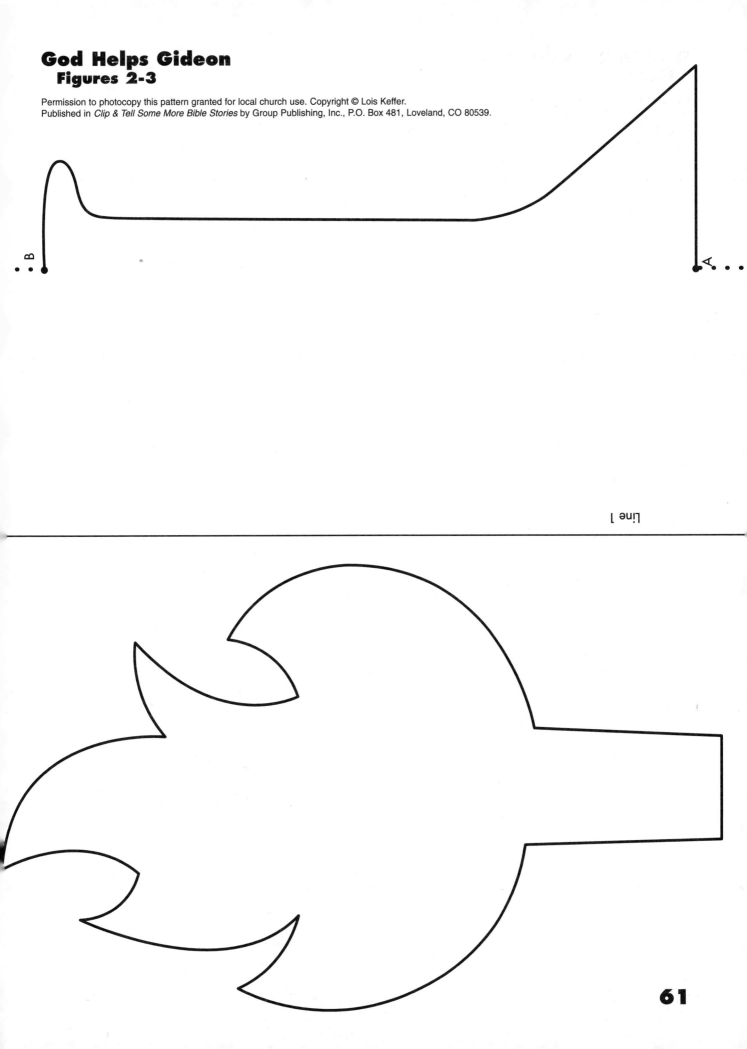

Line 1

God Helps Gideon
Figure 4

Line 2

Line 1

Slit

Line 3

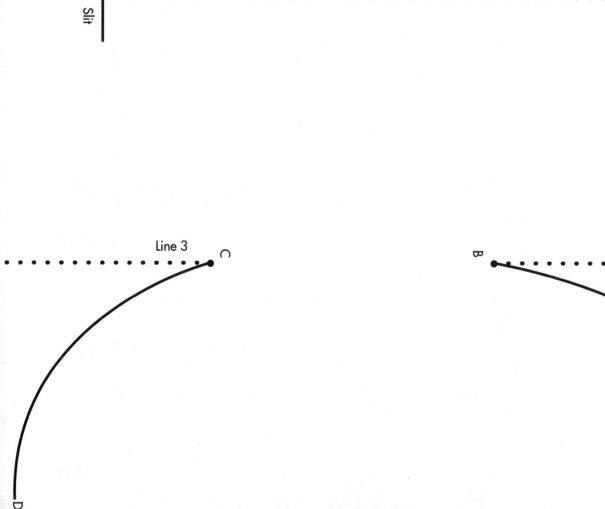

SAMUEL LISTENS TO GOD

PREPARATION

Copy Figures 1-2 (Samuel and the bed) onto beige paper. Copy Figures 3-4 (the ears) onto white paper. You'll need a copy of the ears for each child. The patterns for this story are on pages 65 and 66.

THE STORY

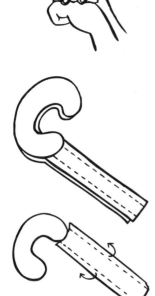

Once long ago, there lived a boy named Samuel.

◺ *Fold Figures 1 and 2 on Line 1 and then cut them apart on Line 2. Set the bed aside.*

Samuel lived in God's house with an old priest named Eli.

✂ *Keeping Samuel folded on Line 1, cut out the circles. Then open the figure.*

Eli was like a father to Samuel.

✂ *Cut around the outline of Samuel. Put a finger through each hole to form Samuel's legs. Make Samuel stand by resting your fingertips on the back of your other hand.*

He taught Samuel how to do all the duties of a priest: how to offer prayers and sacrifices, what to do with the offerings, how to read and write Scripture, and, most important of all—how to listen to God.

◺ *Set Samuel aside. Fold the bed on Line 3 and then set it aside.*

You see, Eli had two sons who should have grown up to serve God and take Eli's place. But they disobeyed God and did terrible things in God's house. And Eli didn't make them stop.

✂ *On Figures 3 and 4, cut the ear pieces apart on the diagonal dotted line. Turn one ear piece over and then put the ear pieces together and cut out both at the same time.*

So God wanted Samuel to be the next priest instead of Eli's sons.

☞ *Set the ear pieces aside.*

One night when Samuel was about twelve years old, he lay sleeping in his bed in the temple.

☞ *Slide two fingers through the circles on Samuel to form his legs. Tuck Samuel into his bed.*

63

But in the middle of the night, someone called out "Samuel!" Samuel scrambled out of his bed and went to see old Eli.

👉 *Make Samuel jump up from his bed and walk across your hand.*

"Here I am," Samuel said.

"I didn't call you," Eli answered. "Go back and lie down."

So Samuel crawled back into his bed.

"Samuel!" called the voice once more.

Samuel got out of bed and went again to see Eli.

👉 *Make Samuel jump up from his bed and walk across your hand.*

"Here I am," he said. "You called me."

"No, I didn't call you," said Eli. "Go back and lie down."

Samuel crawled back into his bed once more.

👉 *Put Samuel back into his bed.*

"Samuel!" said a voice in the darkness.

Samuel got up and went back to see Eli.

👉 *Make Samuel jump up from his bed and walk across your hand.*

Then Eli realized that it was the Lord who was calling Samuel. So he said, "Go back to bed, and if the Lord calls you, say, 'Speak, Lord, for your servant is listening.' "

👉 *Remove your fingers, and put Samuel back into his bed.*

Samuel tingled with excitement.

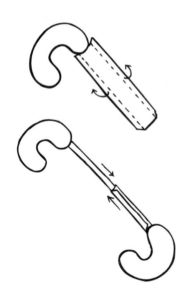

✂ *Cut both ear pieces from A to B and from C to D.*

The Lord had never spoken to him before.

△ *Fold one ear piece headband back on Lines 1 and 2.*

So when he went back to bed this time, he was all ears!

△ *Fold the other ear piece headband back on Lines 1 and 2.*

Sure enough, the Lord called, "Samuel!"

👉 *Slide the ear piece headbands together, one inside the other.*

And Samuel answered, "Speak, for your servant is listening."

👉 *Slip on the ears with the headband going across your forehead.*

God gave Samuel an important message. As Samuel grew up, God continued to talk to him, and Samuel continued to listen. Everyone knew that the words Samuel spoke were true, because Samuel listened to God.

God wants us to listen to him, too. Let's all make Samuel ears as a reminder to listen when we pray.

👉 *Give each child a set of ears. Help kids cut and fold the ears and adjust their headbands so the ears fit snugly. When all the children are wearing their ears, pray a simple prayer asking God to help each child to remember to listen when he or she prays.*

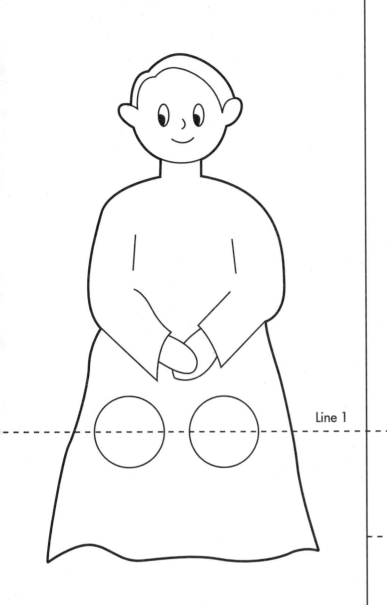

Bed

Line 1

Line 3

Line 2

Samuel Listens to God
Figures 1-2

Permission to photocopy this pattern granted for
local church use. Copyright © Lois Keffer.
Published in *Clip & Tell Some More Bible Stories*
by Group Publishing, Inc., P.O. Box 481,
Loveland, CO 80539.

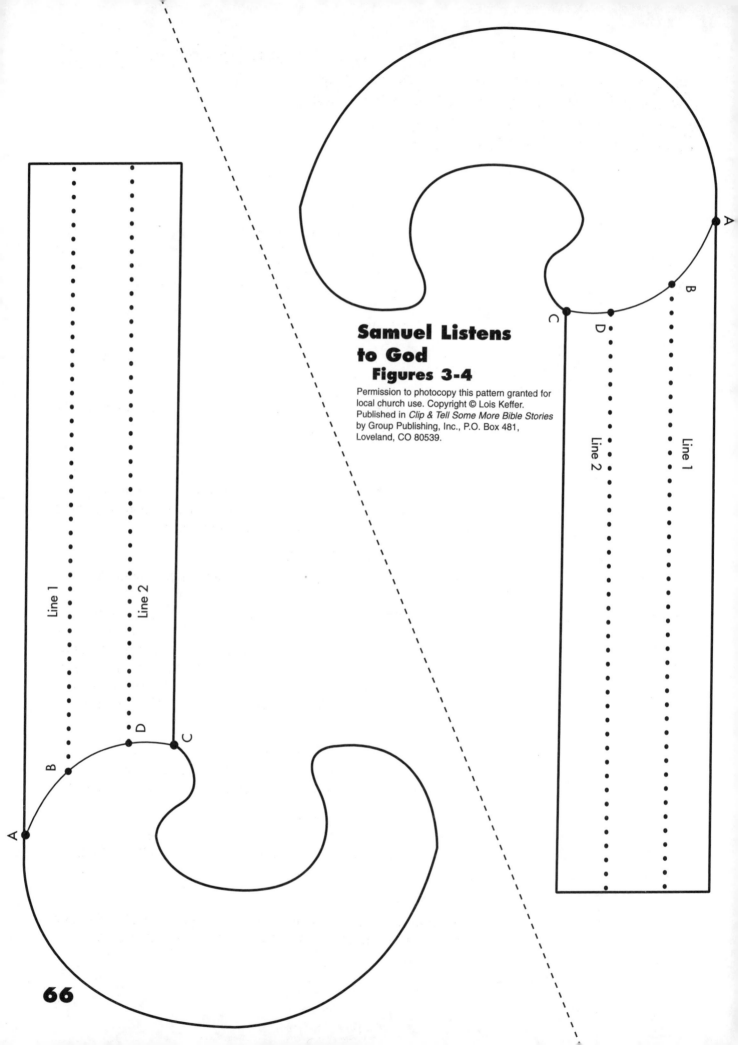

Samuel Listens to God
Figures 3-4

Line 1

Line 2

Line 1

Line 2

1 SAMUEL 25:2-42

ABIGAIL SHARES WITH DAVID

PREPARATION

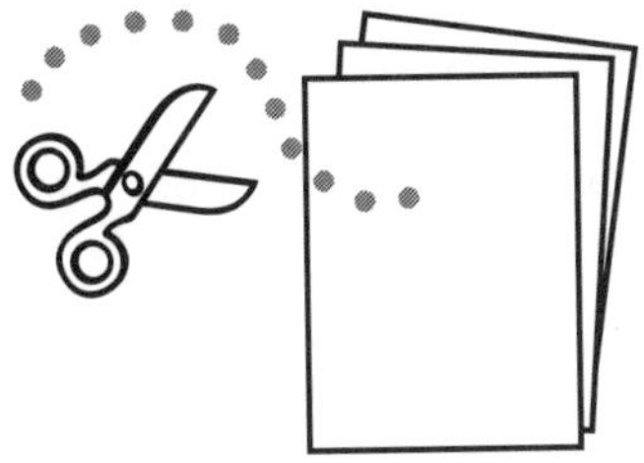

Copy Figures 1-3 (David, the basket, and Abigail) onto heavy beige paper. Copy Figure 4 (the donkeys) onto brown paper. The patterns for this story are on pages 69 and 70. (NOTE: You may want to partially precut the Abigail, David, or donkey figures to save time as you tell the story.)

THE STORY

When King Saul turned away from God, God chose David to be the next king of Israel. When Saul heard this, he became jealous of David and set out to kill him. So David took his fighting men and hid in the mountains.

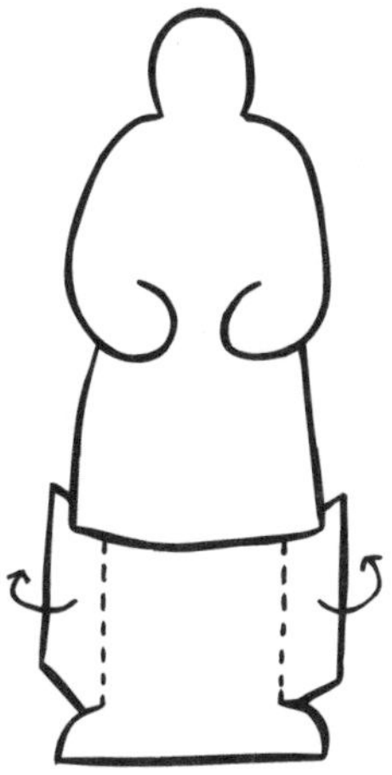

Begin cutting around Figure 1 (David), cutting the hands to A and B.

David and his men camped near the home of a wealthy farmer named Nabal. Day after day, David's men saw Nabal's workers tending sheep in the valleys and on hillsides near David's camp.

Fold back on Lines 1 and 2 to make the figure stand.

David and his men watched over the shepherds and made sure no harm came to them or to the sheep.

When the time came to shear the wool off the sheep, Nabal held a big party. David and his men needed food, so David sent a messenger to Nabal. The messenger said, "Long life and good health to you and your household! I know that it is time to shear the sheep and that you are having a feast. When your shepherds were near us, we took care of them and they didn't lose a single sheep. Now please share with us whatever food you can."

Cut around Figure 2 (the basket).

Though Nabal was very rich, he was also mean and selfish. "Why should I share any of my own food with David?" he answered angrily.

Cut from A to B and from C to D and then fold back the tabs on the dotted lines. Set the basket aside.

The messenger returned to David and told what Nabal had said. David was furious at Nabal's selfishness.

Cut around Figure 3 (Abigail).

In the meantime, Nabal's servants went to Abigail, Nabal's wife, and told her what had happened. Abigail was both beautiful and wise.

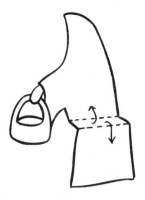

△ *Fold the figure of Abigail up on Line 1 (a valley fold) and down on Line 2 (a mountain fold). Set Abigail aside.*

She quickly packed up bread, wine, roasted grain, raisin cakes, fig cakes, and sheep for roasting and loaded all the food on donkeys.

△ *Fold Figure 4 on Line 1 and cut out both donkeys at once, leaving the area between the donkeys' legs solid.*

Then she mounted a donkey and rode out to meet David.

✂ *Cut the donkeys apart on Line 1. Place the basket on one donkey by folding the tabs backward and slipping them over the donkey's back. Place Abigail on the other donkey so she appears to be riding it.*

When Abigail saw David, she got off her donkey and bowed down before him.

☞ *Take Abigail off the donkey, straighten her to make her stand, and then fold on Lines 1 and 2 again to make her bow.*

"My lord, please listen to me," she said. "My husband Nabal is a wicked man. I did not see the messenger you sent. But when I heard what happened, I loaded these donkeys with food for you and your men. Please forgive Nabal's offense and accept this gift from me."

David accepted the food from Abigail.

☞ *Take the basket off the donkey, and slide it into David's hands.*

"Praise God for keeping me from killing your husband in anger," David said. "Now go home in peace."

When Abigail returned home, she told Nabal about the food she had taken to David and his men. Nabal suddenly became very sick. Just a few days later, he died.

Then David sent word to Abigail and asked her to become his wife. She agreed. And that is how a wise, generous woman came to be the wife of a king.

Nabal was selfish and wanted to keep all his riches. Abigail knew that all good things come from God, and she was happy to share. God wants us to be like Abigail and share the good things he's given us.

Help children remember the story with this simple action rhyme.

Mean old Nabal was as selfish as could be.*(Make a mean face.)*

He wanted all his riches for himself, you see.*(Cross your fists over your heart.)*

But Abigail was generous, kind, and good.*(Hold out one palm and then the other.)*

She was glad to give David lots of food.*(Pretend to hand out food.)*

She knew that good things come from God above *(point to your head and then point to the sky),*

And that when we share, we show God's love!

(Spread your arms wide with your palms up and then make a heart with your arms overhead and your fingertips resting on your head.)

Line 2

Line 1

A

B

A

B

C

D

Line 2

Line 1

**Abigail Shares
With David
Figures 1-3**

Permission to photocopy this pattern granted for
local church use. Copyright © Lois Keffer.
Published in *Clip & Tell Some More Bible Stories*
by Group Publishing, Inc., P.O. Box 481,
Loveland, CO 80539.

**Abigail Shares
With David**
Figure 4

Permission to photocopy this pattern granted for
local church use. Copyright © Lois Keffer.
Published in *Clip & Tell Some More Bible Stories*
by Group Publishing, Inc., P.O. Box 481,
Loveland, CO 80539.

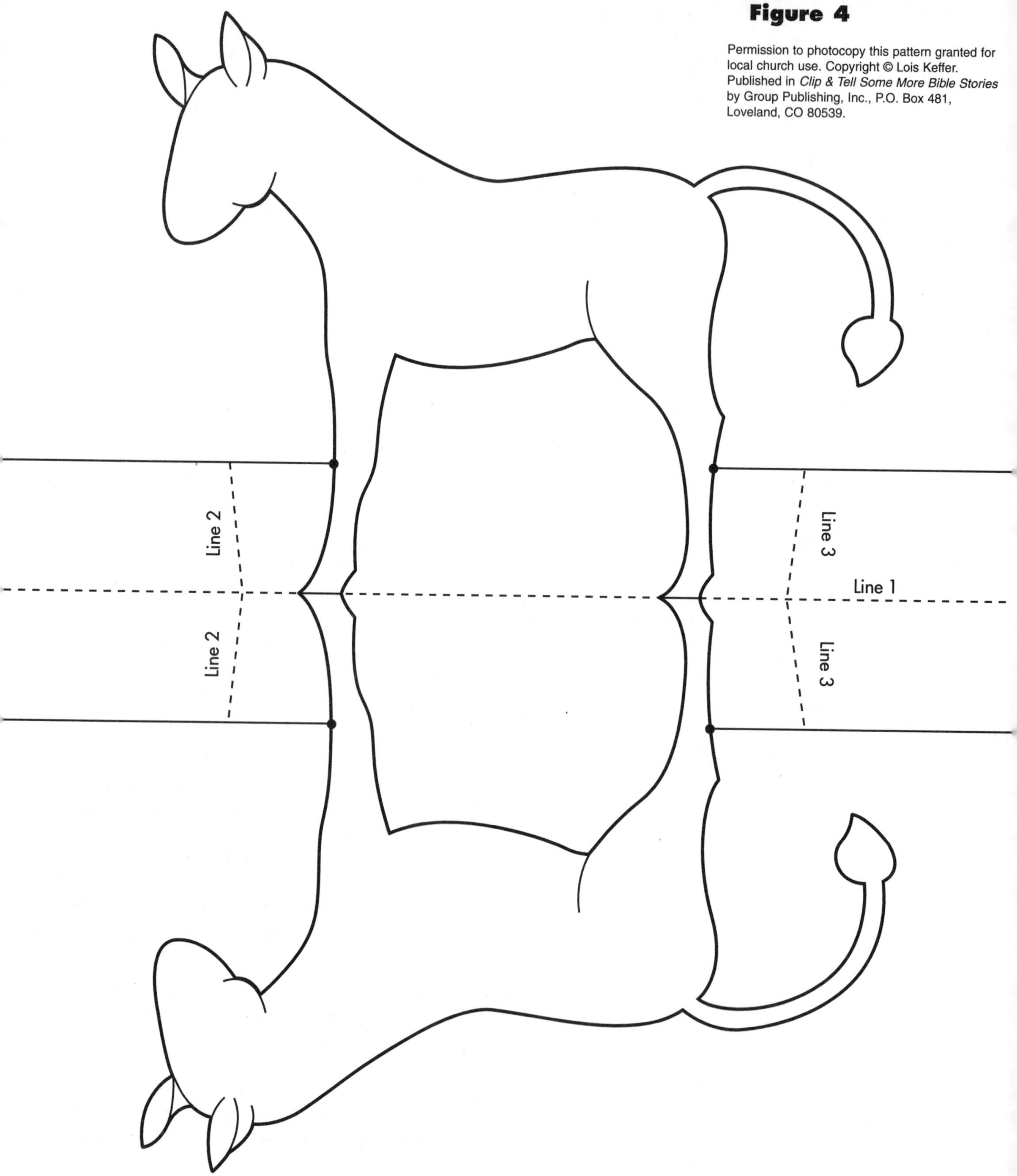

Line 2

Line 2

Line 3

Line 1

Line 3

GOD HEALS NAAMAN

PREPARATION

Copy Figure 1 (Naaman and the river) onto light blue paper. The pattern for this story is on page 73.

THE STORY

Once there lived a great general called Naaman.

△ *Fold Figure 1 in half on Line 1.*

Naaman lived in the country of Aram where he served the king and commanded the whole army.

✂ *Cut from A to B, and open the figure.*

Even though Naaman was brave and strong, there was one battle he could not win.

△ *Fold back on Line 2, so the river is flat (on a table or chair) and children see just the figure of the man.*

You see, Naaman was sick with a terrible disease called leprosy. No one knew how to cure Naaman's disease.

No one, that is, except a little slave girl who served Naaman's wife. The slave girl was from Israel, and she knew that God could do anything. So one day the slave girl said, "If only my master could see God's prophet, he could be cured from his sickness."

Naaman's wife told him what the slave girl had said. Then Naaman went to the king and got permission to go to Israel. First Naaman visited the king of Israel. But the king didn't know what to do for him. Then the prophet Elisha sent a message to the king. The message said, "Send the man to me."

So Naaman set off to find Elisha. When he came to Elisha's house, Elisha didn't even come to the door! Instead he had his servant tell Naaman, "Go wash seven times in the Jordan River, and you will be cured from your disease."

Naaman was furious! "I came all this way!" he shouted. "Surely this prophet can come out and see me and call on his God to cure me. If I wanted to wash in a river, I could have done that in my own country!"

But Naaman's servants pleaded with him to obey Elisha and go wash in the river. "If this prophet had told you to do something hard," they said, "you surely would have done it! But he's only asked you to do something easy. Won't you go wash in the river as he said?"

Finally Naaman agreed. He went down to the Jordan River and waded into the water.

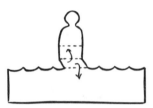 *Display the river and then fold down on Line 2 (a mountain fold) and up on Line 3 (a valley fold) so Naaman appears to be standing in the river.*

Then he dipped into the water seven times. Count them with me!

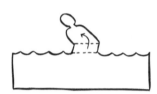 *As children count, fold back on Line 4 and then up again to make it seem that Naaman is dipping under the water.*

One, two, three, four, five, six, seven.

And when he came up out of the water, his skin was completely free of the terrible disease. God had healed him!

Fold the river out of sight and make Naaman stand again.

Naaman and his servants went back to see the prophet Elisha and thanked him. They tried to give gifts to the prophet, but he wouldn't accept them.

Naaman said, "Now I know that the God of Israel is the only true God."

It was a joyful day when Naaman returned to his home, well and strong again. Imagine how he thanked the little girl who told him that God's prophet could cure him!

You may know people who have big problems like Naaman's. Maybe you'd really like to help them, but you don't know how. Well, you can do the very same thing the little slave girl did. You can send them to some-one who knows God. You might send them to a pastor or a teacher or even one of your parents. People who know God can help others learn to know God, too. And you can be the person who points the way.

Let's all think of someone right now who has a problem. Don't say the person's name or what the problem might be out loud—just think of it in your mind. Has everyone thought of someone? Now you pray along silently as I pray out loud.

Dear God, we're thankful that you can solve any problem, big or small. We all know people who have problems, and we're thinking of them right now. Please be with those people and help them as you helped Naaman. And help us to bring these people to you. In Jesus' name, amen.

Now let's celebrate God's goodness with this fun little rhyme. You repeat after me.

One, two, three, four, five, six, seven.

All praise to God who lives in heaven!

Seven, six, five, four, three, two, one.

I'll worship God—he's the only one!

God Heals Naaman
Figure 1

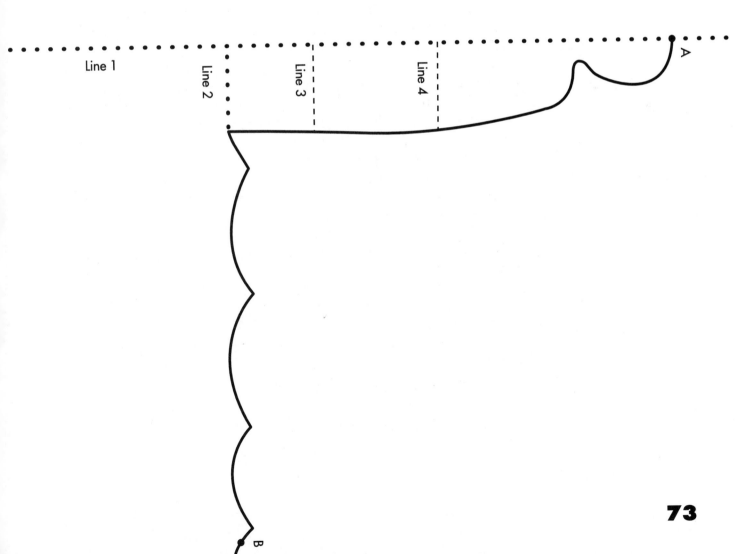

Line 1

Line 2

Line 3

Line 4

A

B

NEW TESTAMENT

JESUS COMES AS A BABY

Copy Figure 1 (Bethlehem) onto dark blue paper. Copy Figures 2 and 3 (the star and baby Jesus) onto light yellow paper. Copy Figures 4 and 5 (Anna and Simeon) onto beige paper. Use a craft knife to open the slits in the hands of Simeon and Anna. The patterns for this story are on pages 79-81.

THE STORY

Long, long ago, God promised his people that he would send a Savior—someone who would set his people free. Israel was just a small country, you see, and sometimes bigger nations with mighty armies would conquer the Israelites and make them slaves or make them pay high taxes.

✂ *Cut Figure 1 from A to B and from C to D.*

The Israelites wanted to be free! And they thought that the Savior God promised would be a great king who would build a strong army and drive out their enemies.

△ *Fold forward on Line 1. Fold back on Lines 2 and 3.*

But God had a different plan. God wanted to set his people free from sin. So instead of sending a great king or general, God sent his own Son, Jesus.

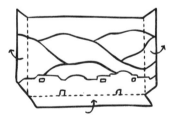

☞ *Stand Bethlehem on a small table or on your lap.*

Instead of being born in a palace, Jesus was born in the little town of Bethlehem where his parents went to pay their taxes.

Jesus was a king, all right, but he didn't want to rule a country—he wanted to rule people's hearts.

✂ *Cut around Figure 2 (the star) and then cut to A and B.*

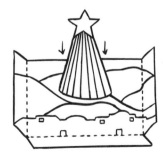

Very few people knew that the little baby who was born in Bethlehem's stable was really God's own Son. Some shepherds knew, because as they were out on the hillsides watching their sheep, an angel appeared in the sky and announced Jesus' birth.

△ *Fold the star back on Lines 1 and 2 and then slide it into place over Bethlehem.*

Some wise men knew, because they saw a special star in the heavens. They followed the star to Bethlehem and worshiped Jesus.

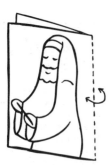

✂ *Cut out Figure 3 (baby Jesus), and show him to the children.*

And a kind old man and a kind old woman in Jerusalem knew, because they prayed to God all the time and God told them about baby Jesus.

◺ *Fold the beige paper in half and cut out Figures 4 and 5 (Anna and Simeon) simultaneously.*

You see, when Jesus was eight days old, Joseph and Mary took him to the temple in Jerusalem.

☞ *Hold up Simeon, and slide baby Jesus into the slit in Simeon's hands.*

An old man named Simeon was at the temple that day, praying to God. When Simeon saw baby Jesus and his parents, he took the baby in his arms and praised God. "Now I may rest in peace because you have shown me your salvation!" Simeon prayed.

☞ *Hold up Anna, and slide baby Jesus into the slit in her hands.*

A sweet old widow named Anna was at the temple that day, too. She came to the temple nearly every day and prayed from morning 'til night. When she saw baby Jesus, she gave thanks to God and told everyone standing nearby that this child was the Savior they'd been waiting for.

Let's see. How many people knew that Jesus was the Savior? The shepherds, the wise men, and Simeon and Anna. And now you know, too! Let's sing a special song to welcome baby Jesus.

Teach children this song to the tune of "Mulberry Bush."

Jesus is born in Bethlehem, Bethlehem, Bethlehem.
Jesus is born in Bethlehem. Oh, hear the angels sing.

Shepherds and wise men, welcome him, welcome him, welcome him.
Shepherds and wise men, welcome him. What wonderful gifts they bring!

Simeon and Anna, praise the Lord, praise the Lord, praise the Lord.
Simeon and Anna, praise the Lord, for you have seen the King.

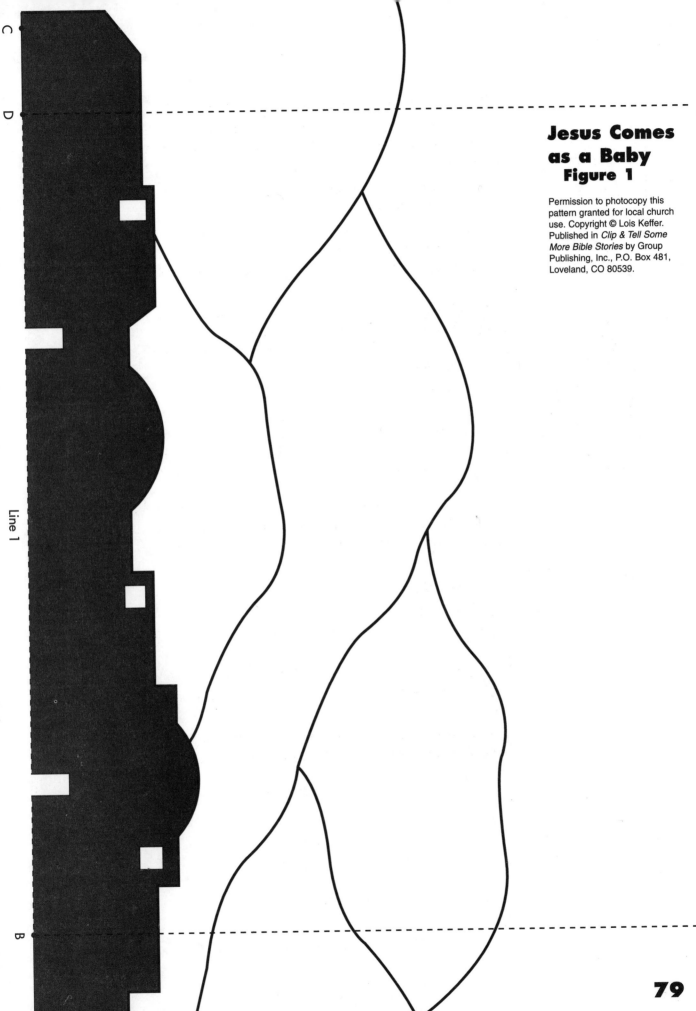

Jesus Comes as a Baby
Figure 1

C

D

Line 1

B

A

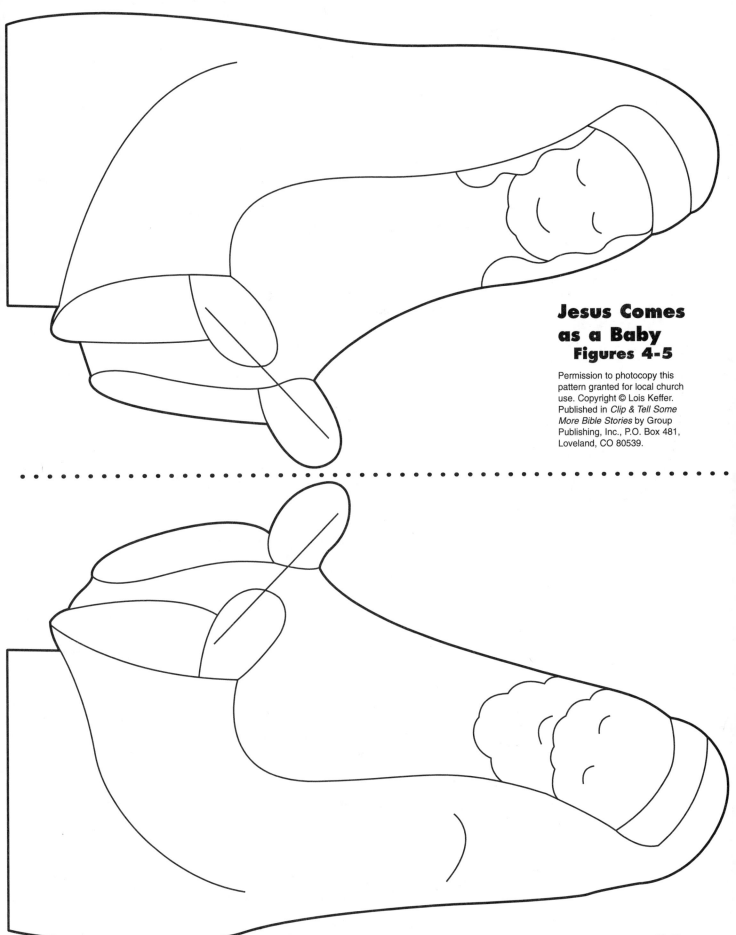

**Jesus Comes
as a Baby**
Figures 4-5

Permission to photocopy this
pattern granted for local church
use. Copyright © Lois Keffer.
Published in *Clip & Tell Some
More Bible Stories* by Group
Publishing, Inc., P.O. Box 481,
Loveland, CO 80539.

JOHN BAPTIZES JESUS

PREPARATION

Copy Figure 1 (John) onto blue paper. Copy Figure 2 (the dove) onto white paper. The patterns for this story are on pages 84 and 85.

THE STORY

John the Baptist lived in the desert.

Fold Figure 1 in half on Line 1.

What do you think it would be like to live in a desert? What would you eat if you lived in the desert? John ate locusts and wild honey. I would like wild honey, wouldn't you? But locusts are bugs—I'm not sure I'd like to eat bugs.

Cut from A to C, unfold the figure, and fold forward on Line 2.

God called John to live in the desert and gave John a very special job to do. John's job was to help people learn about God and announce that Jesus was coming. An Old Testament prophet told about John hundreds of years before John was even born. The prophet said that there would be "a voice of one calling in the desert, 'Prepare the way for the Lord.' "

So John began to preach, and believe it or not, people came out to the desert to hear him. "Repent!" he said. That means to be sorry for the wrong things you've done and to decide not to do them anymore. John also said, "The kingdom of heaven is near." John knew that God was about to do something very special on earth.

Refold Figure 1 on Line 1. Cut from B to C and unfold.

Many people who believed John's message and really wanted to live for God went to the Jordan River where John baptized them. John gently dipped them into the river and then raised them back up again. By being baptized, people showed that they wanted to turn away from lives of sin and live lives that would please God.

"I baptize you with water," John said, "but someone is coming who is much more powerful than I am. The one who is coming after me is so great that I'm not even fit to tie his sandals! He will baptize you with fire and with the Holy Spirit."

Do you know who John was talking about? Jesus!

△ *Fold Figure 2 on the center line and begin cutting the outline of the dove.*

Jesus was even more special than John, because Jesus was God's own Son. Jesus came to earth to be our Savior and take away the sins of the whole world. That's why John was so surprised when Jesus came and asked to be baptized.

John said, "You're the one who should baptize me!"

But Jesus understood that there was a special reason for him to be baptized. So John finally agreed, and he gently dipped Jesus into the water of the Jordan River.

When Jesus came up out of the water, something wonderful happened!

 ☞ *Open the dove, and pretend to "fly" it toward the children.*

Heaven opened, and the Spirit of God came down like a dove. A voice from heaven said, "This is my Son. I am very pleased with him."

After his baptism, Jesus was ready to begin preaching, teaching, and healing people. But John was put in prison, because the leaders of the country didn't want to repent of their sins and live for God. They didn't want to hear John's preaching, so they put him in prison to keep him quiet.

However, the people who had listened to John were ready to listen to Jesus and to accept Jesus as God's Son. John had done a wonderful job of getting people ready to hear Jesus' message.

You may wish to use this opportunity to teach children your church's view of baptism. Simply say, "We still baptize people today." Then explain how your church practices baptism.

Teach children this song to the tune of "When Johnny Comes Marching Home."

Oh, John the Baptist told the people, "Repent—today."
He taught them to turn away from sin and live God's way.
He baptized the people and Jesus, too.
That's the job that God gave him to do.
Now we'll all follow God, and we'll do
What is right
From day 'til night.
Boom! Boom! Boom!
(repeat)

Line 1

Line 2

A

C

B

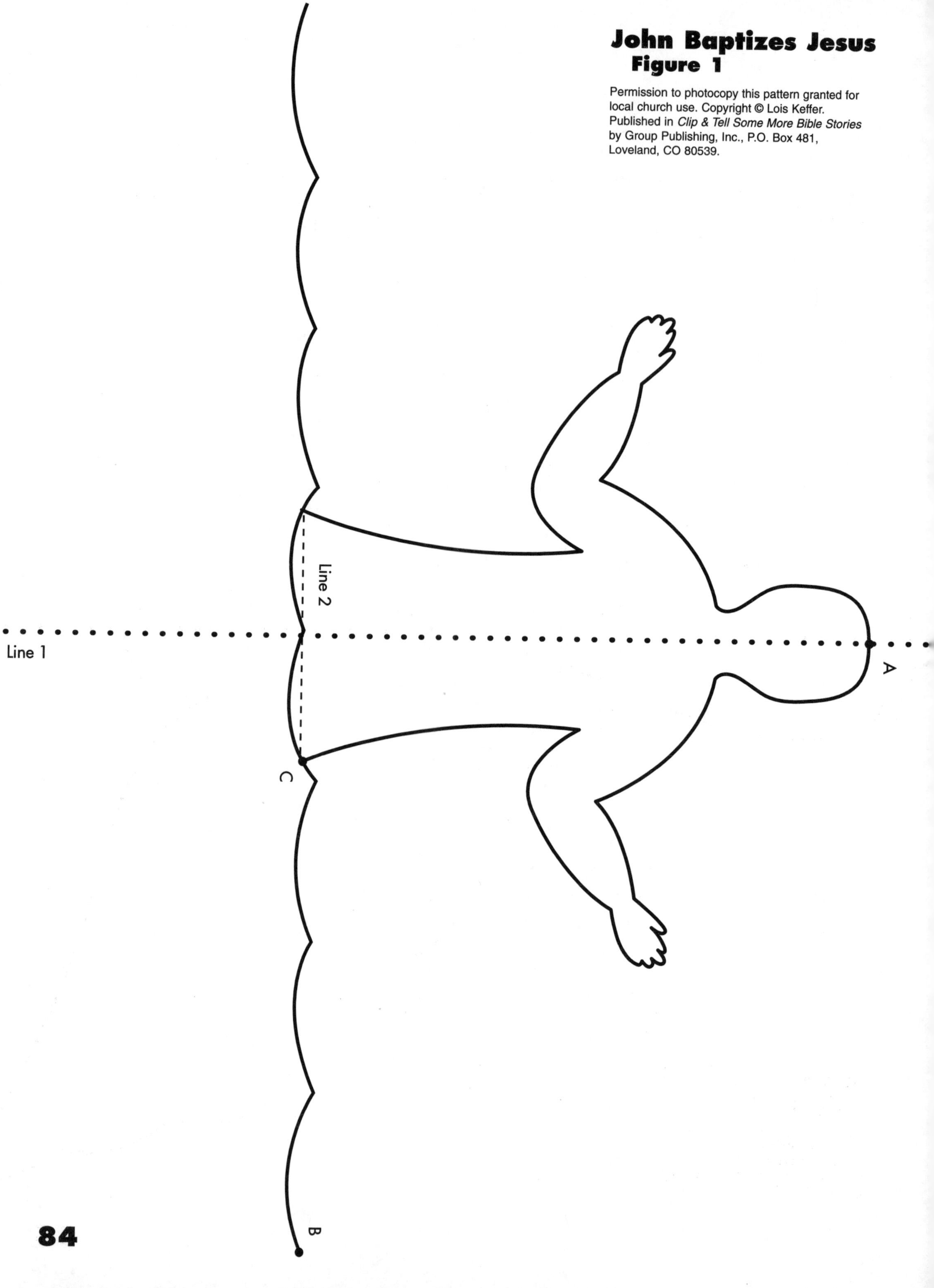

John Baptizes Jesus
Figure 2

JESUS TEACHES US

Copy Figure 1 (the city) onto dark blue paper. Copy Figure 2 (the mouth) and Figure 3 (the heart and fists) onto red paper. You'll also need a bag of pretzels and a flashlight or a sheet of bright yellow paper. The patterns for this story are on pages 88-90.

THE STORY

One day, Jesus gathered his followers on a mountainside and began to teach.

"You are the salt of the earth," Jesus said.

What does salt do?

Let's think of some salty foods—pretzels, chips, and crackers. All those things wouldn't be nearly as tasty without salt. Here—I have a salty pretzel for each of you.

☞ *Pass out pretzels.*

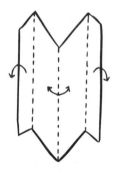

To be like salt, we need to make things better. When someone is hurting, we can help that person feel better. When someone is lonely, we can be caring friends. We can do all those things when we have Jesus' love in our hearts.

△ *Fold Figure 1 forward on Line 4 (a valley fold). Then fold back on Lines 1 and 7 (mountain folds). Cut the sides and bottoms (the solid lines) of the windows that are on Lines 1 and 7.*

Jesus also said, "You are the light of the world." Sometimes our world is dark with sin.

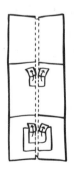

△ *Open the folds on Lines 1 and 7. Fold the windows up on the dotted lines. Fold back on Lines 2 and 6. Cut the sides and bottoms of the doors and windows on Lines 2 and 6.*

People hurt each other when their hearts are filled with sin.

△ *Open the folds on Lines 2 and 6. Fold the windows and doors up on the dotted lines. Fold back on Lines 3 and 5. Cut the sides and bottoms of the windows on Lines 3 and 5.*

When Jesus comes into our lives, he takes that sin away and replaces it with the light of his love.

△ *Open the folds on Lines 3 and 5. Fold the windows back up on the*

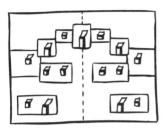

dotted lines. Fold back on Line 4. Cut the sides and bottom of the door.

Have you ever been in a really dark place? Hearts filled with sin are dark like that. But what happens when someone lights a candle?

△ *Open the fold on Line 4. Fold the door back on the dotted line. Darken the room, and shine a flashlight through the doors and windows of the city. If you can't darken the room, place a sheet of bright yellow paper behind the city.*

Even one candle makes a huge difference in a dark room. A person with Jesus' love in his or her heart can make a big difference, too.

Jesus said, "A city on a hill cannot be hidden." When we ask Jesus to fill our hearts with his love, we glow just like this city. Then we're obeying Jesus' command to let our light shine.

△ *Fold Figure 2 in half on Line 1. Cut from A to B.*

Jesus said, "Do not swear at all." Swearing means using God's name in the wrong way. Why do people do that?

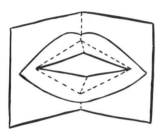

△ *Fold both backward and forward on Lines 2 and 3.*

Sometimes people don't even think about the words they're saying.

☞ *Open the lips. Bend slightly forward on Line 1, and pull the folds of the lips forward. When you bend forward on Line 1 and then flatten the paper, the lips will open and close as if they're talking.*

But it's a bad habit. And bad habits can be broken. If you're in the habit of using God's name in the wrong way, you can ask Jesus to help you break that habit. Jesus wants us to be careful with our words.

☞ *Use the talking mouth to speak to several children by name with messages such as "You're nice!" "I like you!" and "I'm glad you're here today!"*

Be sure to use your mouth for good things!

△ *Fold Figure 3 in half on Line 1. Cut from A to B.*

Jesus said, "Love your enemies." What is an enemy?

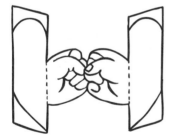

✂ *Cut from C to D. Open the figure, and display the fists.*

Sometimes we don't even know how people get to be our enemies. We never hurt them or did anything bad to them, but they don't like us. They might make fun of us or do mean things. Can you love people who are mean to you?

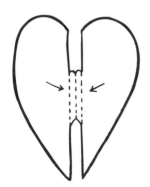

△ *Fold back on Line 1. Cut around the outline of the heart. Fold up on Line 1 (a mountain fold). Fold back on Lines 2 and 3 to bring the halves of the heart together.*

Let's sing a song that will help you remember what Jesus taught.

Teach children this song to the tune of "Ten Little Indians."

We're the light of the world, so glow and shi-ne.
Speak only good words all of the ti-me.
Love your enemies, and you'll do fi-ne,
When your heart is filled with God's love.

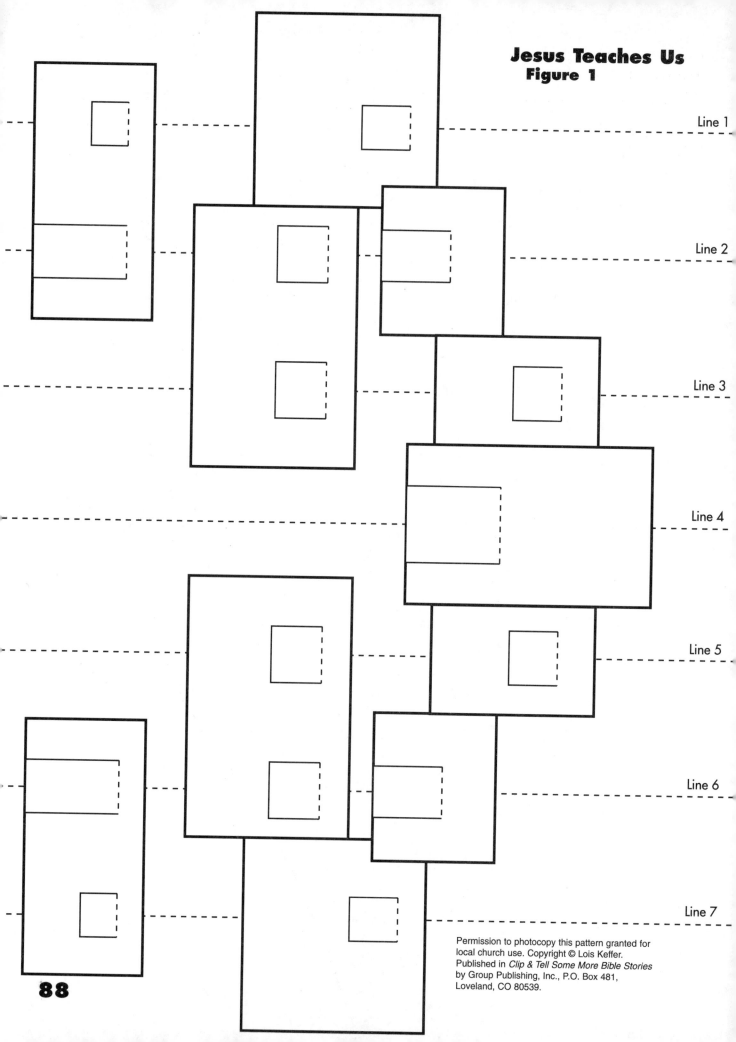

Jesus Teaches Us
Figure 1

Line 1

Line 2

Line 3

Line 4

Line 5

Line 6

Line 7

Jesus Teaches Us
Figure 2

Line 1

Line 2

Line 3

A

B

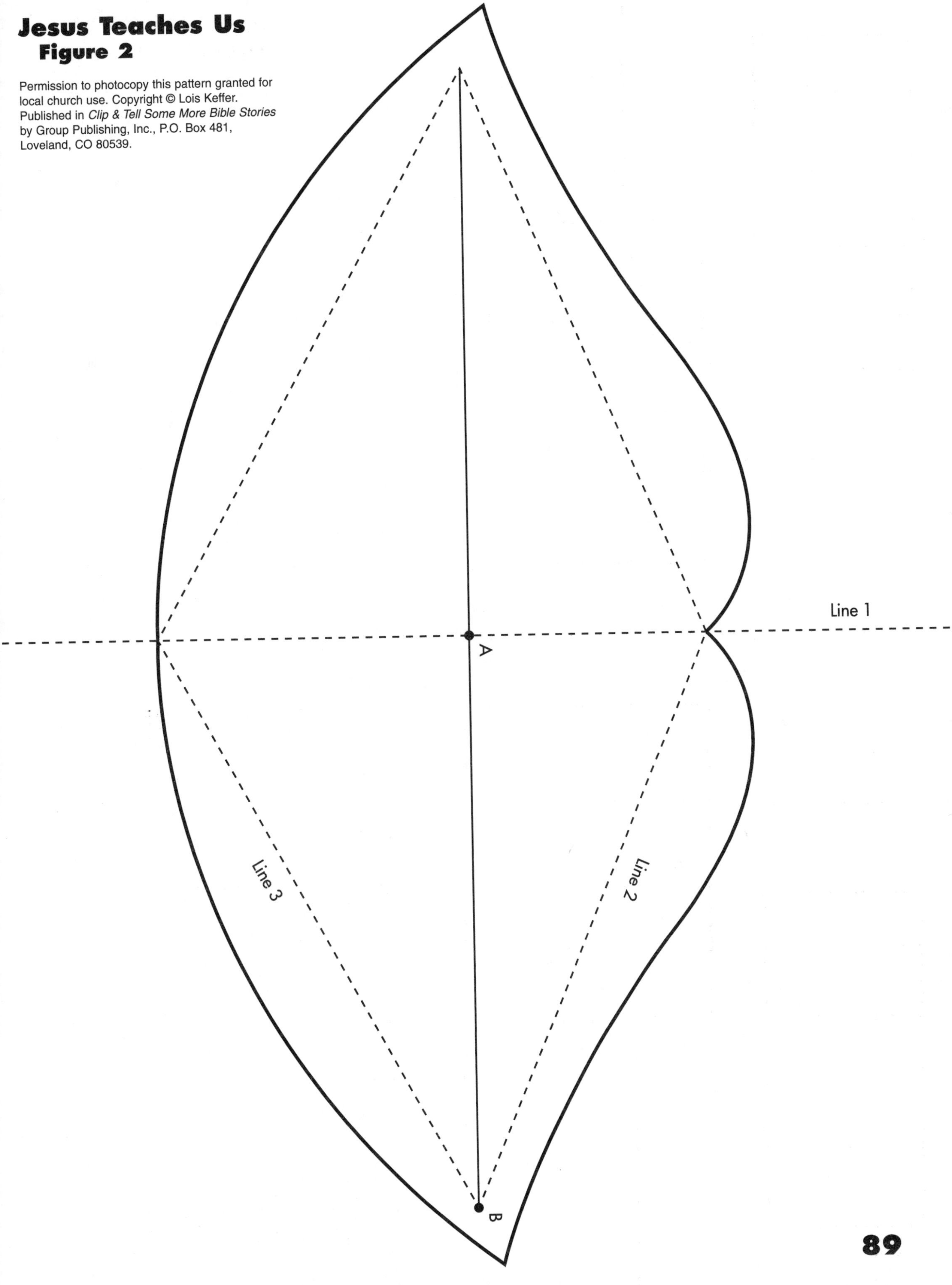

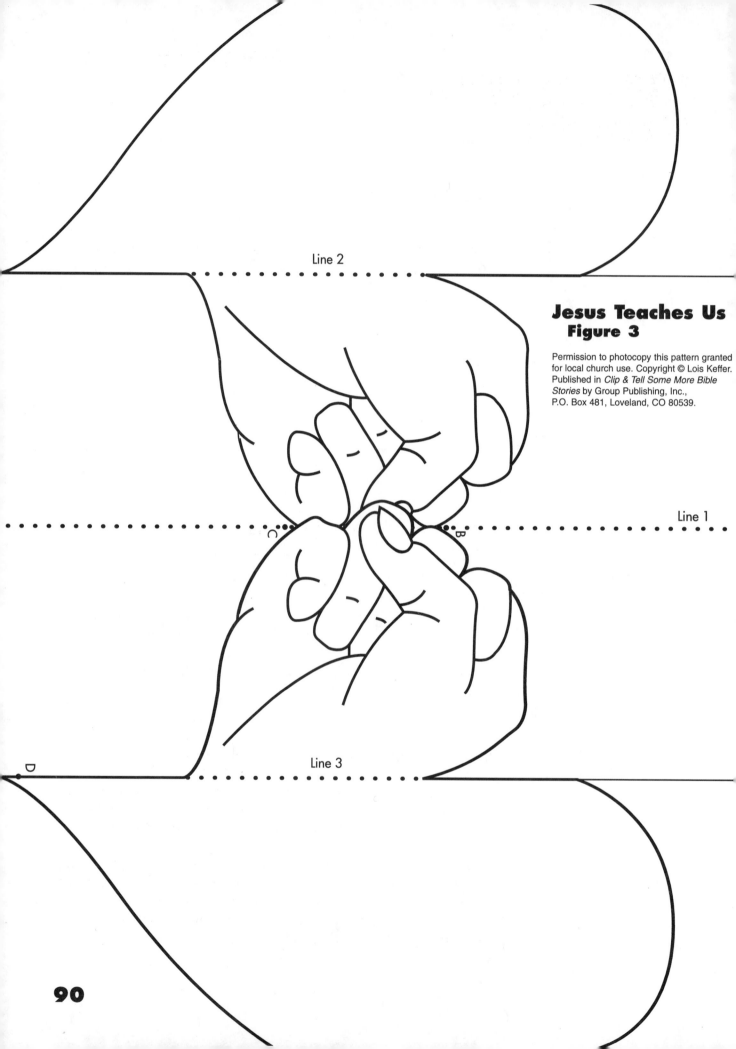

Line 2

Jesus Teaches Us
Figure 3

Line 1

C

B

Line 3

D

THE LORD'S PRAYER

PREPARATION

Copy Figure 1 (the crown containing the word "God") onto gold paper. Copy Figure 2 (the bread and the fruit) onto beige paper. Copy Figure 3 (the word "sorry") onto green paper. Copy Figure 4 (the octagonal sign) onto red paper. The patterns for this story are on pages 94-96.

THE STORY

✂ *Begin cutting around Figure 1.*

One day after Jesus had been praying, one of his disciples said, "Lord, teach us to pray." The disciples knew that Jesus prayed often. If prayer was important to Jesus, they wanted to know how to pray, too!

So Jesus said, "When you pray, pray like this.

Our Father in heaven, hallowed be your name."

When we say those words, we're talking to God.

☞ *Display Figure 1, and point to the word "God."*

God is the maker of our world and our whole universe. We can talk to God just as Jesus did.

"Hallowed be your name" means that God's name is special and deserves to be honored and praised. Can you think of some songs we sing that honor and praise God?

Let's say that much of the prayer together. "Our Father in heaven, hallowed be your name."

Have children repeat.

The next part of the prayer Jesus taught his disciples goes like this: "Your kingdom come, your will be done on earth as it is in heaven." A kingdom is a place that's ruled by a king. That's why there's a crown in this picture. God is king of all the world, and God is king in the hearts of those who love him. If you love God, make a big heart by raising your arms over your head and pointing your fingertips down to your head.

God's kingdom comes when people who love God do the things God wants them to do. When we're loving, helpful, and kind, we bring God's kingdom to earth. Every time we pray this prayer, it's like crowning God the king of our hearts. Let's say that line of the prayer together. "Your kingdom come, your will be done on earth as it is in heaven."

✂ *Have children repeat. Begin cutting around Figure 2. To cut quickly, cut loosely around the drawing rather than cutting each shape.*

Next, Jesus prayed, "Give us today our daily bread." Raise your hand if you eat bread every day. What other things do you eat every day?

☞ *Display Figure 2.*

What do you see in this picture besides bread?

Jesus wants us to ask God to give us all the things we need every day—food, a place to live, clothes, and people to take care of us. Jesus wants us to remember that all the things we need come from God. Let's say that line of Jesus' prayer together. "Give us today our daily bread."

Have children repeat. Begin cutting loosely around Figure 3.

Then Jesus prayed, "Forgive us our debts, as we also have forgiven our debtors." Jesus knew that we need to be forgiven for the wrong things we do every day.

☞ *Display Figure 3.*

We don't always do wrong things on purpose—sometimes we just slip up. Even then we need to tell God we're sorry.

But there's another part, too. We need to forgive other people for the wrong things they do to us. That's not always easy. In fact, it can be downright hard! If someone hurts us or makes us mad, we don't want to forgive them. But that's our job. That's what God expects. If God is willing to forgive us, we need to be willing to forgive others. Let's say that line of the prayer Jesus taught his disciples. "Forgive us our debts, as we also have forgiven our debtors."

Have children repeat. Begin cutting around Figure 4.

Finally, Jesus prayed, "Lead us not into temptation, but deliver us from the evil one." Temptation is when we really want to do something but we know we shouldn't. We might be tempted to tell a lie to stay out of trouble. We might be tempted to say something nasty about a person we don't like. Sometimes I'm tempted to drive my car a little too fast.

What's tempting to you?

Every day is filled with tempting things, but Jesus' prayer asks for God's help to stay away from temptation.

☞ *Display Figure 4.*

What does this shape remind you of? That's right—it looks like a stop sign. When we want to do something wrong, God can help us say, "Stop!"

The evil one is the devil. He wants to do wrong things. But God can help us beat the devil and do what's right. Let's say this last line of Jesus' prayer together. "Lead us not into temptation, but deliver us from the evil one."

Have children repeat.

There! Now you've learned about the prayer Jesus taught his disciples.

When you pray to God, you can pray for these same things Jesus did. God loves to hear your prayers! Let's pray right now.

Dear Lord, thank you for teaching us how to pray. Help us remember to talk to you each day. In Jesus' name, amen.

You may want to help children make booklets of the Lord's Prayer by reducing the four patterns and stapling them together in booklets. Let kids color the pages and keep the booklets as prayer reminders.

Permission to photocopy this pattern granted for local church use. Copyright © Lois Keffer. Published in *Clip & Tell Some More Bible Stories* by Group Publishing, Inc., P.O. Box 481, Loveland, CO 80539.

"Our Father in heaven, hallowed be your name. Your kingdom come, your will be done on earth as it is in heaven."

(Matthew 6:9-10)

GOD

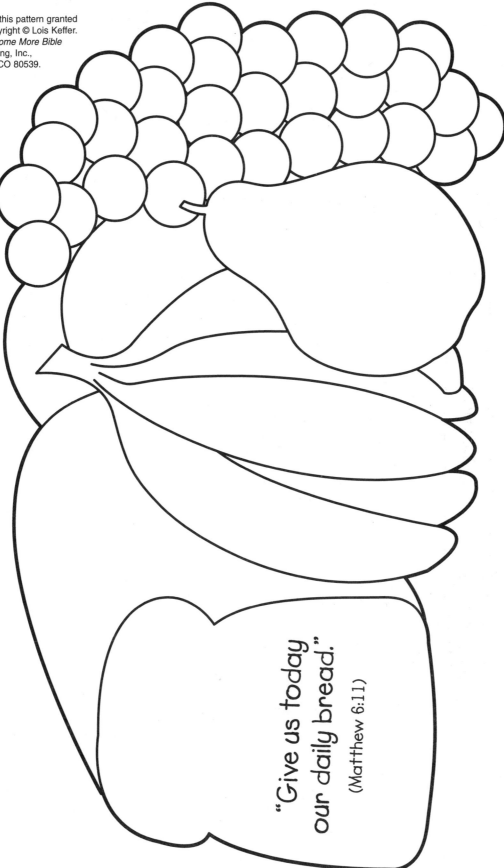

"Give us today our daily bread." (Matthew 6:11)

"And lead us not into temptation, but deliver us from the evil one."

(Matthew 6:13)

**The Lord's Prayer
Figures 3-4**

Permission to photocopy this pattern granted for local church use. Copyright © Lois Keffer. Published in *Clip & Tell Some More Bible Stories* by Group Publishing, Inc., P.O. Box 481, Loveland, CO 80539.

SORRY

"Forgive us our debts, as we also have forgiven our debtors."
(Matthew 6:12)

THE LORD'S SUPPER

PREPARATION

Copy Figure 1 (the feet) onto beige paper. Copy Figure 2 (the bread) onto brown paper. Copy Figure 3 (the cup of wine) onto purple paper. The patterns for this story are on pages 99-101.

THE STORY

Jesus wanted to share a special meal with his disciples. You see, Jesus knew that his time to live on earth was almost finished and that this was the last meal he would share with his closest friends.

So he sent Peter and John ahead to get the meal ready.

When Jesus and the rest of the disciples arrived, there was no servant to wash their feet. In Bible times, the roads were very dusty. When someone came to visit, a servant would greet the guests and wash the dust off their feet. The disciples must have looked at each other and thought, "I'm not going to wash anyone's feet. I'm not a servant, after all!"

Fold Figure 1 in half on the dotted line, and cut from A to B.

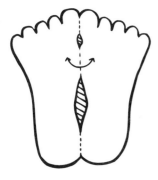

Then Jesus surprised everyone. He got up from the table, wrapped a towel around his waist, poured water into a bowl, and began to wash the feet of his disciples.

Open Figure 1, and rub the feet as if you were washing them.

Jesus' friends were shocked and embarrassed. None of them had been willing to do a servant's job, so Jesus—the Son of God—did it.

When Jesus finished, he said, "Do you understand what I've done for you? Even though you call me Lord and Teacher, I have washed your feet. I have set an example for you by being willing to serve. If you do as I have done, you'll be blessed."

Fold Figure 2 in half on the dotted line, and cut from A to B.

After Jesus had washed everyone's feet, he took his place at the table.

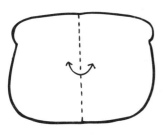

Open Figure 2.

Then he picked up the bread and said, "This is my body that will be given for you. Do this to remember me." And Jesus gave each of the men a piece of bread to eat.

Fold Figure 3 in half on the dotted line, and cut from A to B.

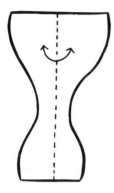

Then Jesus picked up the cup.

☞ *Open Figure 3.*

He said, "This is my blood that will be poured out so that your sins can be forgiven."

The disciples didn't understand what Jesus meant. But we understand. We know that Jesus was about to give his life on the cross to pay for the sins of the whole world.

Today when we celebrate the Lord's Supper (or Communion), we remember that Jesus was willing to give his life so that our sins could be forgiven.

You may wish to use this opportunity to teach children how your church celebrates the Lord's Supper. You might let children break pieces off a loaf of French bread and drink small cups of grape juice.

The Lord's Supper
Figure 1

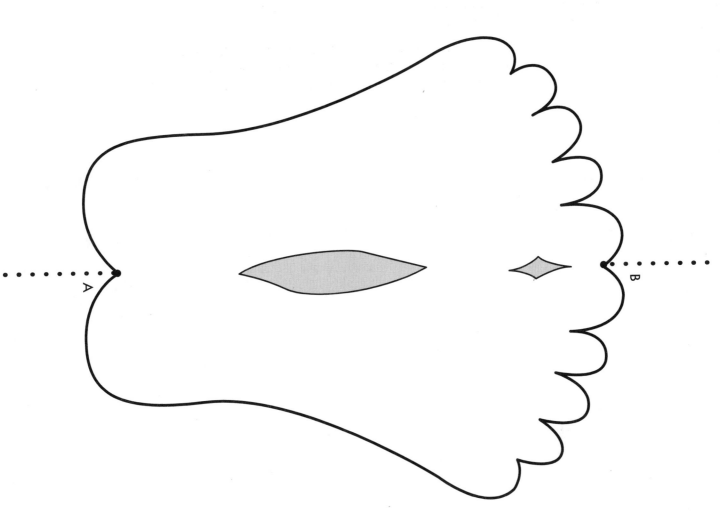

The Lord's Supper
Figure 2

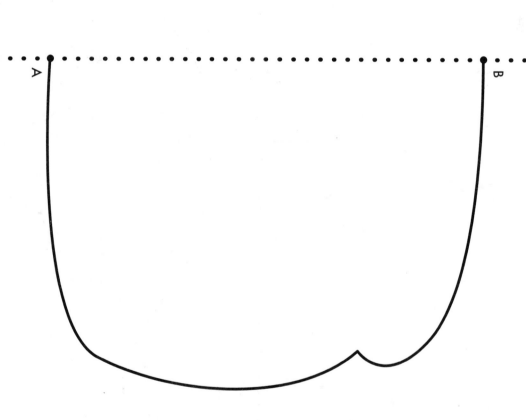

A

B

The Lord's Supper
Figure 3

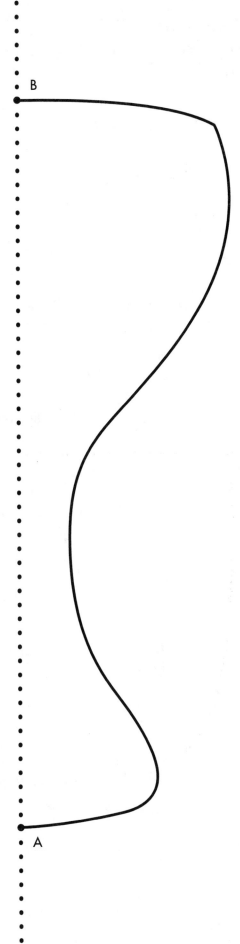

B

A

FROM GETHSEMANE TO THE CROSS

PREPARATION

Copy Figure 1 (Jesus in the garden) onto dark green paper. Copy Figure 2 (the crown of thorns) onto brown paper. Copy Figure 3 (the cross and the gift) onto shiny silver wrapping paper. The patterns for this story are on pages 104-106.

(NOTE: You may want to partially precut Figures 1 and 2 to make your storytelling time flow more smoothly.)

THE STORY

The disciples could tell that Jesus was sad. They had eaten the Passover meal together and sung a hymn of thanks to God. Then they walked to a grove of olive trees where there was a beautiful garden.

Begin cutting around Figure 1.

Jesus said to his followers, "Sit here while I go over there and pray." So most of the disciples sat down to rest. They had never seen Jesus look so sad and troubled. Jesus asked Peter, James, and John to go on to the garden with him.

"I'm so sad," Jesus told them. "Stay here and keep watch with me." It was late at night, and the disciples were tired.

Display Figure 1.

Jesus went on further into the garden to pray. After a little while, he came back and found his disciples sound asleep.

"Couldn't you stay awake for even one hour?" Jesus asked. The sleepy disciples were embarrassed. Then Jesus went back to the garden and prayed a while longer. When he came back to the disciples, he found them asleep once more. Jesus went and prayed a third time while the sleepy disciples dozed off.

This time when Jesus came back, he woke his disciples. "Are you still sleeping?" he asked. "Look, here comes the man who will betray me!"

The disciples jumped up and rubbed their eyes in astonishment. There was Judas leading a crowd of people armed with swords and clubs. Guards arrested Jesus and led him away. The terrified disciples scattered in every direction. How could this be happening?

Fold Figure 2 in half on the dotted line. Cut from A to B and from C to D.

The guards took Jesus to be questioned by the high priest. The high priest tried to make it sound like Jesus had done something wrong.

People lied about Jesus and made fun of him. Finally they took him to Pilate, the Roman governor.

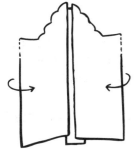

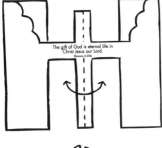

The gift of God is eternal life in
Christ Jesus our Lord.
(Romans 6:23b)

△ *Fold Figure 3 in half on the dotted line. Cut from A to B and from C to D.*

After questioning Jesus, Pilate said, "This man has committed no crime." But the crowd shouted, "Crucify him!"

So the Roman guards took Jesus and placed a crown of thorns on his head.

☞ *Display Figure 2.*

Then they led him to a hill outside of town and hung him on a cross.

☞ *Open Figure 3 and display the cross.*

Jesus didn't have to die. He was the Son of God—he could have done a miracle and set himself free. But Jesus wanted to give his life. Do you know why? Because he loves us so much. Jesus knew that only he could pay the price for the wrong things we do.

△ *Fold Figure 3 in half again and cut from E to F. Open the figure and fold the panels inward so they cover the cross and create a "gift."*

Jesus' death was a gift to us. It means that we can have our sins forgiven and live with him in heaven someday. That's a pretty terrific gift, right?

And do you know what else is wonderful? Jesus' death is not the end of the story. Because three days later...who can tell me what happened?

That's right! Jesus rose from the dead. But that's another story for another day. Let's stop and thank Jesus right now for what he did for us on the cross.

Dear Jesus, we know that you're the Son of God and that you could have done a miracle instead of dying on the cross. Thank you for loving us so much that you were willing to die for us. Thank you for your wonderful gifts of forgiveness and life in heaven. We love you, Jesus. Amen.

You may want to let each child cut and fold Figure 3, the cross and the gift. Encourage children to learn Romans 6:23b, the verse that's printed on the cross.

**From Gethsemane
to the Cross
Figure 1**

From Gethsemane
to the Cross
Figure 3

The gift of God is eternal life
in Christ Jesus our Lord.
(Romans 6:23b)

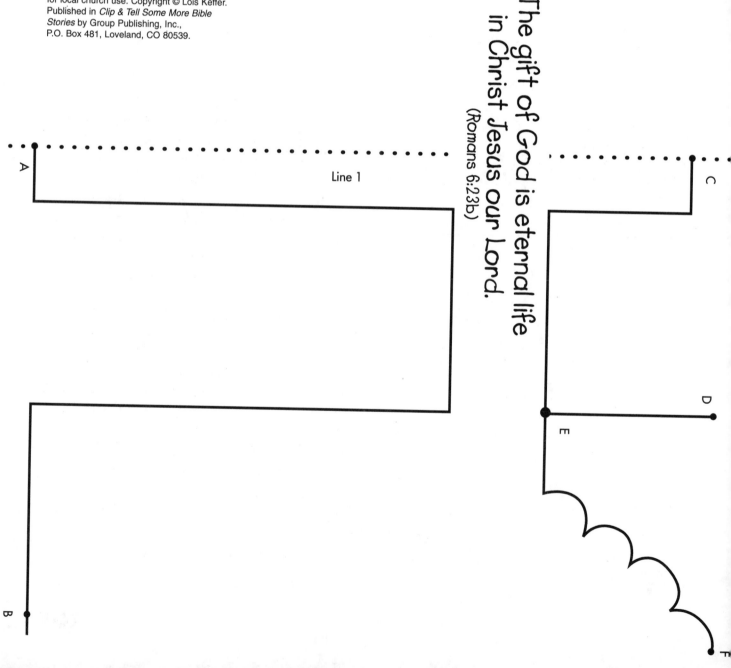

Line 1

JESUS IS ALIVE

PREPARATION

Copy Figure 1 (three men on a road) onto beige paper. Copy Figures 2-3 (Jesus at the table, the circle of disciples) onto gray paper. Copy Figure 4 (Jesus rising into a cloud) onto white paper. The patterns for this story are on pages 109-111.

THE STORY

After Jesus died on the cross, his friends felt so sad and scared. Their Lord and friend was gone! They didn't know what to do.

✂ *Cut out Figure 1 on the two diagonal lines.*

A man named Joseph took Jesus' body and laid it in a tomb. A huge stone was placed in front of the tomb, and Roman guards kept watch.

◭ *Fold Figure 1 back on Line 1. Cut from A to B and from C to D. Fold up on the remaining two dotted lines, and pinch the figure of the men so they stand up and appear to be walking down a road.*

The next Sunday morning, two of Jesus' friends were walking down the road that led to the village of Emmaus (ee-MAY-us). As they walked, they were talking about all of the terrible things that had happened to Jesus. They could hardly believe that Jesus had died.

All at once, a third man joined them. "What are you talking about?" he asked.

"Are you the only visitor to Jerusalem who doesn't know the things that have happened?" one of the friends asked.

"What things?" asked the newcomer.

"About Jesus of Nazareth," answered the other friend. "He was a prophet of God, but the chief priests and rulers had him put to death. Then this morning some women went to his tomb. His body wasn't there! The women saw angels who said that Jesus was alive. So some of our other friends went to the tomb. Sure enough, Jesus' body had disappeared!"

◭ *Fold Figures 2 and 3 in half on Line 1. Cut the 2 figures apart on Line 2. Set Figure 3 (the circle of disciples) aside.*

The stranger began to explain to the two friends that the Bible told that all of these things would happen.

✂ *Cut Figure 2 from A to B. Then cut away the shaded area.*

107

When they reached the village of Emmaus, the friends asked the stranger to eat with them.

◩ *Open Figure 2.*

So they sat down at a table, and the stranger gave thanks for the bread and then broke it and gave it to them. Suddenly, they realized who the stranger was. Then he disappeared.

☞ *Set Figure 2 aside.*

The friends looked at each other in amazement. "It was Jesus!" they cried. "It's true! He has risen!" The two men jumped up and hurried back to Jerusalem to share the good news.

✂ *Cut Figure 4 from A to B, from B to C, and from C to D. Fold back on Line 1, and display the figure of Jesus.*

Over the next few weeks, Jesus appeared to his disciples many times. He explained to them that Scripture taught that he would die and then rise again.

✂ *Cut Figure 3 from C to D and then open it.*

One day Jesus met his disciples on a hillside. He gave them a special job to do. "Go into all the world," Jesus said, "and tell everyone the good news."

Then, suddenly, Jesus began to rise into the sky

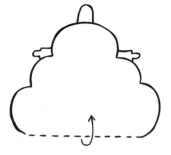

✂ *Cut Figure 4 around the outline of the cloud and then raise the figure and gradually fold the cloud up until it covers Jesus.*

until he disappeared into the clouds.

As the disciples continued looking up, an angel suddenly appeared beside them. "Why do you stand here looking into the sky?" the angel asked. "Jesus has been taken up into heaven. One day he will come back again just as he left."

Isn't that exciting? Jesus will come back again someday! And when that happens, he will take his followers to heaven where we will live with him forever! Let's learn a song that will remind us that if we love Jesus and live for him, we'll go to heaven someday.

Teach children this song to the tune of "Jesus Loves Me."

> Jesus died on a cross long ago.
> But he didn't stay in the tomb, I know.
> He rose to heaven so far away,
> And he's coming back someday!
>
> I'll live for Jesus, I'll live for Jesus,
> I'll live for Jesus and go to heaven someday.

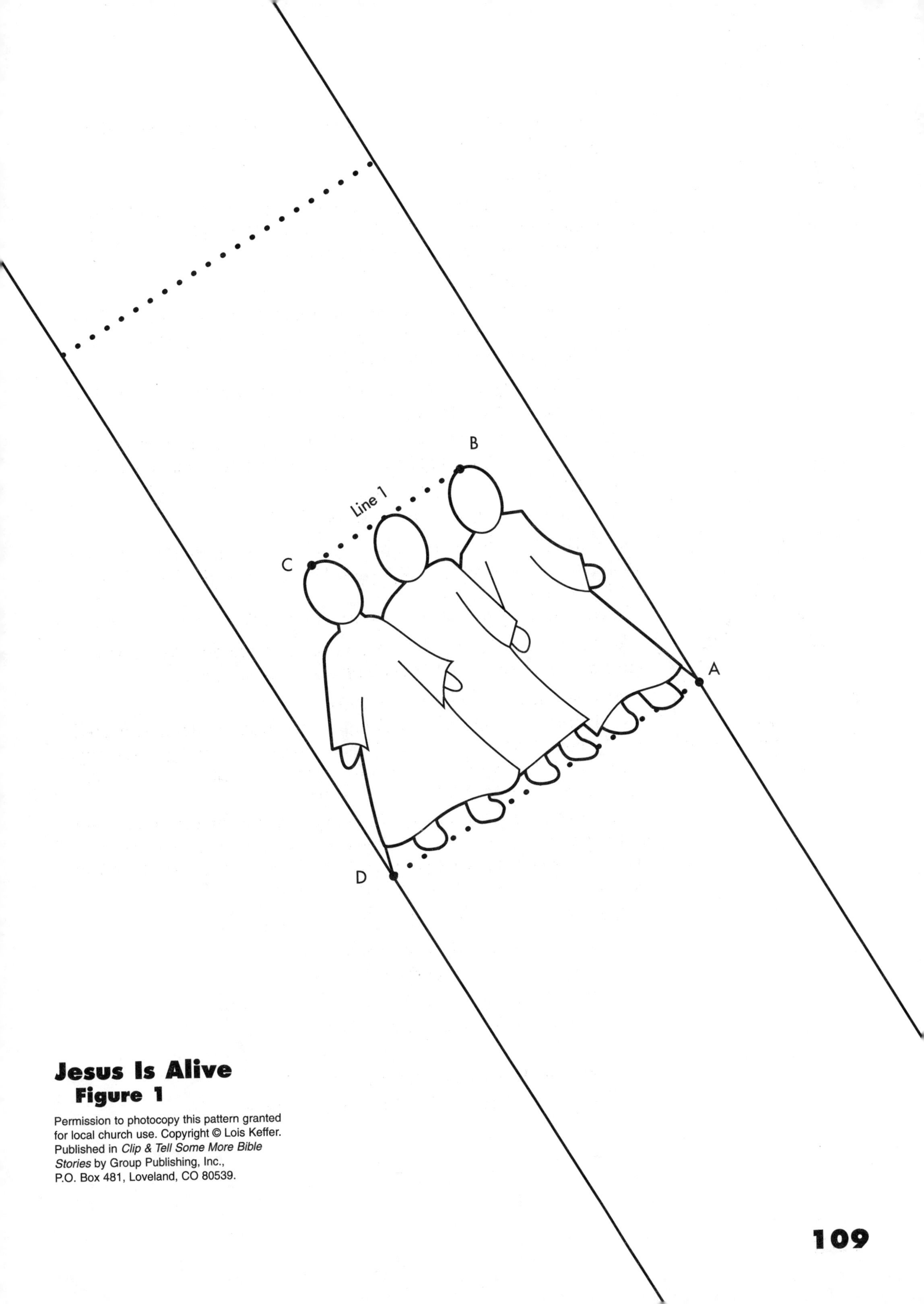

Line 1

B

C

A

D

Jesus Is Alive
Figure 1

Jesus Is Alive
Figures 2-3

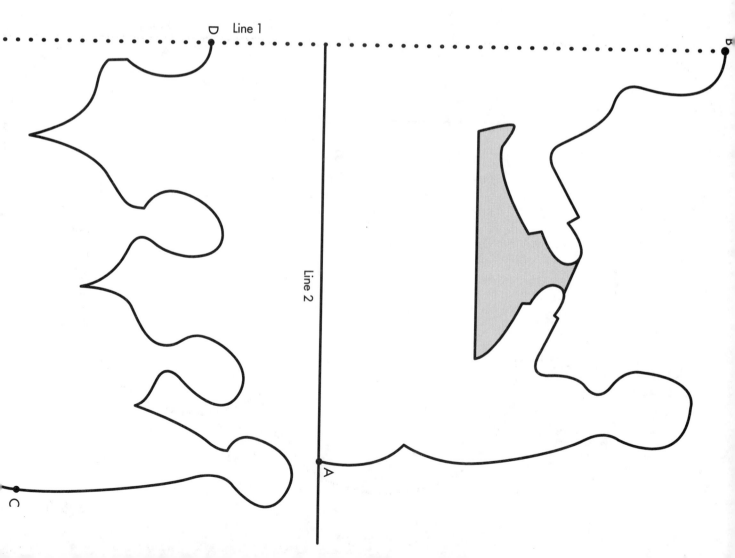

Line 1

Line 2

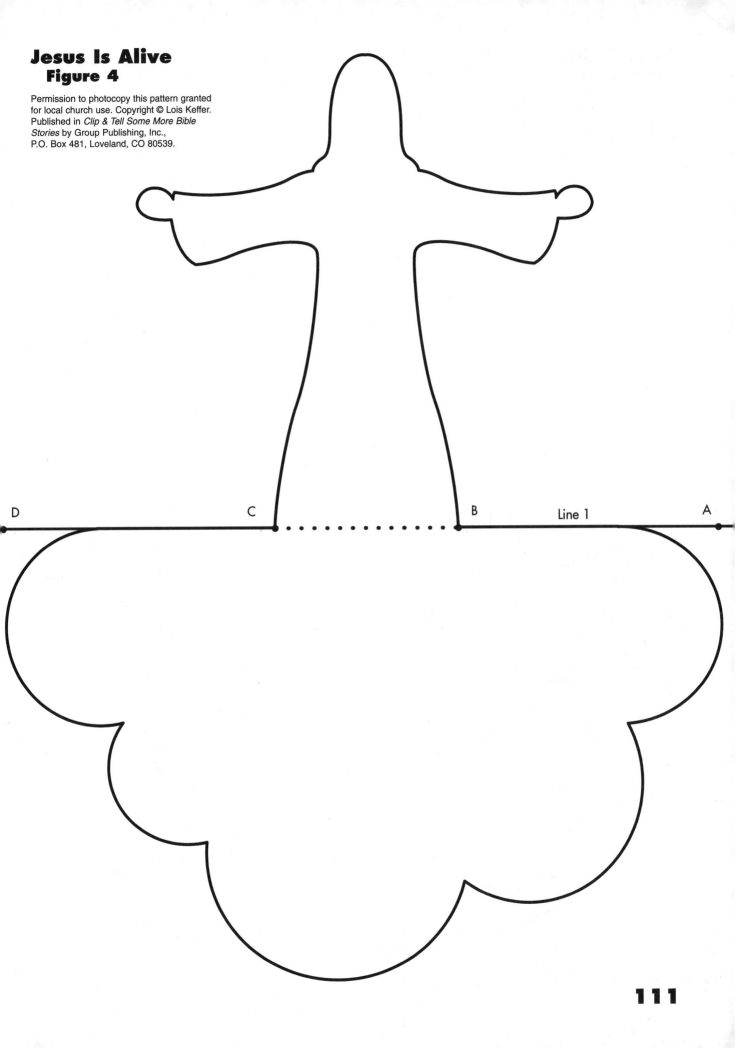

Jesus Is Alive
Figure 4

D   C   B   Line 1   A